DIABETIC AIR FRYER COOKBOOK FOR BEGINNERS 2023:

1500 Days Fresh, Balanced and Healthy Recipes Book for Pre Diabetic, Type 2 Diabetes and Managing Blood Sugar

Darren Medina

Copyright © 2023 Darren Medina
All rights reserved

No part of this publication may be reproduced or distributed in any form or by any means, electronic or mechanical, scanning, photocopying, recording, or otherwise, without prior written permission from the publisher.

Limit of Liability / Disclaimer of Warranty: The Publisher and the author are not licensed physician, medical professional, or practitioner and offers no medical counseling, treatments, or diagnoses. The Publisher and the author make no warranties with respect to the completeness and accuracy of the contents of this work. The content presented herein has not been evaluated by the U.S. Food and Drug Administration, and it is not intended to diagnose or cure any disease. This book isn't intended as a substitute for medical advice as physicians. Full medical clearance from a licensed physician should be obtained before beginning any diet. The advice and strategies contained herein may not be suitable for every situation. Neither the Publisher nor the author claims no responsibility to any person or entity for any liability, damage, or loss caused directly or indirectly as a result of the use, application, or interpretation of the information presented in this work.

All the nutritional information contained in this book is provided for informational purposes only. The information is based on the specific brands, measurements, and ingredients used to make the recipe. Therefore, the nutritional information in this work in no way is intended to be a guarantee of the actual nutritional value of the recipe made by the reader. The publisher and the author will not be responsible for any damages resulting in the reliance of the reader on the nutritional information.

The Publisher publishes its books in a variety of electronic, audio, and print formats. Some content that appears in print may not be available in electronic or audiobooks, and vice versa.

Table of contents

What to Eat and Avoid 6
Breakfast Recipes 12
Chicken and Mushrooms Muffins 12
Paprika Meatballs 12
Carrot Tots 12
Parsley Meatballs 12
Cottage Cheese Eggs 13
Spinach Pie 13
Cod Balls 13
Stuffed Tortillas 14
Fried Feta 14
Carrot Rolls 14
Oregano Eggs 15
Coconut Pancakes 15
Turmeric Eggs 15
Vanilla Toasts 15
Garlic Eggs 16
Apricot Fritters 16
Kale Cakes 16
Thyme Muffins 16
Beef Rolls 17
Avocado Cups 17
Cheese Sandwich 17
Chicken Chimichangas 18
Asparagus Omelette 18
Nutmeg Eggs 18
Potato Sticks 19
Cilantro Casserole 19
Cherry Tomato Pizzas 19
Fish Quesadillas 19
Gyros 20
Coriander Chicken Fillets 20
Beef and Eggs 20
Chicken Pockets 21
Meat Roll 21
Avocado Canoes 21
Wrapped Chicken 21
Broccoli and Sauce Bites 22
Wonton Crab Meat 22
Oregano and Chicken Meatballs 22
Crushed Eggs 22
Paprika Beef Bars 23

Side Dishes 26
Sweet Potato Fries 26
Curry Fries 26
Dill Potato 26
Nutmeg Mushrooms 26
Cauliflower Mix 27
Turmeric Eggplant Fries 27
Beef Wraps 27
Hot Cakes 27
Broccoli Wings 28
Chili Wedges 28
Cinnamon Apples 28
Thyme Asparagus 28
Parsley Kebabs 29
Ginger Squash 29
Black Pepper Brussels Sprout Halves 29
Soy Sauce Rice 29
Chili Eggplant Coins 30
Radish Hash 30
Garlic Green Beans 30
Chili Turnips 30
Avocado Patties 31
Garlic Tempeh 31
Garlic Cauliflower 31
Dill Broccoli Rice 31
Paprika Cauliflower Rice 32
Zucchini Burgers 32
Parsley Zucchini 32
Appetizer Garlic Bulbs 32
Cilantro and Chickpea Fritters 33
Buffalo Style Broccoli 33
Garlic Asparagus 33
Fragrant Buns 33
Thyme Spaghetti Squash 34
Garlic and Carrot Puree 34
Sage Shredded Cabbage 34
Lemon Purple Cabbage 34
Coriander Portobello Caps 34
Cumin Brussels Sprouts 35
Ginger Plantains 35
Turmeric Cabbage Wedges 35

Fish and Seafood 38
Garlic Shrimps 38
Cod Patties 38

Coriander Lobster Tails	38
Paprika Crab Cakes	38
Italian Seasoning Shrimps	39
Garlic Mussels	39
Coriander Tilapia Fillets	39
Lime Salmon	39
Chili Cod en Papilote	40
Spinach Cod	40
Coriander Tilapia Sticks	40
Tender Mackerel	40
Cumin Catfish	41
Chili Crab Bites	41
Garlic Kampung Fish	41
Nutmeg Tilapia	41
Cumin Sea Bass	42
Cilantro Cod	42
Turmeric Calamari Rings	42
Dill Squids	42
Chili Cod Fillets	43
Cod Balls	43
Tilapia Cream	43
Garlic Seabass	43
Curry Shrimps	44
Nutmeg Scallops	44
Cinnamon Shrimps	44
Rosemary Shrimps	44
Nutmeg Bites	45
Paprika Scallops	45
Fish Spring Rolls	45
Onion Lobsters	45
Oregano Scallops	46
Lime Snapper	46
Lime Dorado	46
Olives and Cod	46
Cayenne Calamari Rings	46
Coriander Sardines	47
Cumin Grilled Sardines	47
Paprika and Basil Mussels	47
Fenugreek Halibut	47
Onion Clams	48
Parsley Crayfish	48
Calamari and Sweet Potato Balls	48
Basil Cod	48
Sweet and Sour Cod	49
Zucchini Sardines	49
Garlic Fish Cakes	49
Chili Fish Tacos	50
Coconut Snapper	50
Poultry	**52**
Lime Chicken	52
Paprika Chicken Drumsticks	52
Chili Pepper Chicken Meatballs	52
Nutmeg Tenders	52
Tomato Wings	53
Italian Seasonings Chicken Thighs	53
Rosemary Whole Chicken	53
Cumin Chicken Breast	53
Parsley Liver Pate	53
Sage Turkey	54
Chives Patties	54
Chicken Breast Boats	54
Onion Chicken	54
Garlic Chicken	55
Oregano Chicken Fillets	55
Marjoram Chicken Shred	55
Spicy Chicken	55
Coated Chicken	55
Yellow Fillets	56
Egg Chicken Fillets	56
Chicken and Kalamata Olives	56
Tender Chicken Strips	56
Greens Wraps	57
Mustard Chicken Tenders	57
Cucumber and Chicken Sandwich	57
Yogurt Chicken Wings	57
Jalapeno Chicken Tights	58
Celery Chicken Thighs	58
Almond Chicken Tenders	58
Tender Chicken Breast	58
Oregano Chicken Sausage	59
Thyme and Garlic Whole Chicken	59
Tomato Chicken Wings	59
Chicken and Onion Bowl	59
Chicken and Asparagus	59
Greek Style Chicken Breast	60
Fenugreek and Dill Chicken	60
Oats Chicken Balls	60
Hot Chili Flakes Chicken	60

Dill Chicken Cutlets 61
Chicken and Tofu Pizza 61
Coriander Duck Breast 61
Oregano Duck Drumsticks 61
Fragrant Whole Chicken 61
Coconut Duck Cream 62
Garlic Duck Meatballs 62
Cayenne Pepper Duck Wings 62
Mustard and Mayo Chicken 62
Spinach and Turkey Mix 63
Chili Poppers 63

Vegetable Meals 66
Cilantro Corn on Cobs 66
Lime Broccoli 66
Carrot Mix 66
Chili Squash 66
Garlic Cauliflower Head 67
Coriander Asparagus 67
Turmeric Cauliflower Florets 67
Fenugreek Mushroom Caps 67
Eggplant Rounds 67
Black Pepper White Beans 68
Sweet Potato Bites 68
Zucchini Bites 68
Ginger Pineapple 68
Crunchy Mushrooms 68
Thyme Green Beans 69
Tofu and Sweet Potatoes 69
Salty Zucchini 69
Garlic Patties 69
Crunchy Eggplants 70
Sweet Potato Tots 70
Tomatillos Salsa 70
Cinnamon Baby Carrots 70
Dill Sweet Potatoes 70
Pumpkin Fries 71
Green Beans Hash 71
Yogurt Zucchini 71
Okra and Garlic Balls 71
Broccoli Fries 71
Cinnamon Apple Wedges 72
Paprika Slices 72
Roasted Jalapeno 72
Lemongrass Bites 72

Beans Peppers 73
Asparagus Fries 73
Zucchini Cubes 73
Chickpea Balls 73
Cilantro Cakes 74
Coconut Cucumbers 74
Parsley Artichoke Hearts 74
Sweet Potato Croquettes 74
Garlic Snap Peas 75
Onion Cakes 75
Mushroom Steak 75
Tofu Burgers 75
Spinach Rolls 76
Stuffed Zucchini 76
Beans Balls 76
Cheese Chickpeas 76
Onion Quesadillas 77
Cauliflower Fritters 77
Turmeric Corn 77
Beans Muffins 77
Arugula Salad 78
Cashew Pizza 78
Dill Parsnip 78

Desserts 80
Vegetable Bars 80
Sweet Zucchini Pie 80
Chocolate Muffins 80
Matcha Cookies 80
Vanilla Bombs 81
Coconut Sandwich 81
Cinnamon Cookies 81
Walnut Cookies 82
Cocoa Cookies 82
Vanilla Clouds 82
Almond Clouds 82
Pecan Cookies 83
Cinnamon Yucca Fries 83
Almond Biscuits 83
Blackberry Skewers 83
Tasty Fries 84

RECIPE INDEX 85

What to Eat and Avoid

Meat, Poultry, and Fish

What to eat	Enjoy occasionally	What to avoid
- Turkey breast (skinless) - Turkey thighs (skinless) - Chicken breast (skinless) - Chicken fillet - Cornish hens (skinless) - Cod (fresh, frozen) - Flounder - Haddock - Halibut - Trout - Lox - Tuna (fresh, canned in water) - Herring - Salmon - Catfish - Sardines - Clams - Crabs - Lobsters - Scallops - Shrimps - Ostrich - Duck (skinless, boneless) - Beef (T-bone, sirloin, tenderloin, steak, ribs) - Pork (center loin chop, tenderloin) - Lamb roast (lean)	- Ground beef - Beef short ribs - Beef prime ribs - Pork cutlet - Ground beef - Ground chicken	- Fried chicken - Chicken skin - Pork spareribs - Pork sausages - Ground pork - Processed sandwich meat - Hot dogs - Bacon - Deep-fried fish

Nuts and Seeds

What to eat	Enjoy occasionally	What to avoid
- Almonds - Walnuts - Pistachios - Pumpkin seeds - Flaxseeds - Cashew	- Chia seeds - Peanuts	- Nuts coated in salt

Vegetables

What to eat
- Artichoke
- Arugula
- Asparagus
- Bok choy
- Broccoli
- Brussels sprouts
- Cauliflower
- Celery
- Eggplant
- Green beans
- Split peas
- Lettuce
- Peppers
- Rhubarb
- Snow peas
- Spinach

Enjoy occasionally
- Tomatillos
- Beetroots
- Carrots, raw
- Collard greens
- Corn
- Green peas
- Mushrooms
- Baked sweet potatoes

What to avoid
- Pickles
- Sauerkraut
- Canned vegetables
- French fries
- Potatoes
- Corn kernels

Beans and Legumes

What to eat
- Edamame beans
- Black beans
- Broad beans
- Great northern beans
- Lentils
- Mung beans
- Navy beans
- Pinto beans
- Lentils

Enjoy occasionally
- Canned beans (salt-free)
- Black beans

Dairy products

What to eat
- Fat-free cheese
- Low-fat cottage cheese
- Grated Parmesan
- Almond milk
- Fat-free milk
- Fermented yogurt
- Skimmed milk

What to avoid
- American cheese
- Cheddar cheese
- Monterey jack cheese
- Swiss cheese
- Chocolate milk
- Ice cream
- Full fat milk
- Full-fat cream

Fruits and Berries

What to eat	What to avoid
- Fresh fruits - Frozen/canned fruits (sugar-free) - Sugar-free - Raspberries - Blueberries - Strawberries	- Chewy fruit rolls - Regular jam - Regular jelly - Canned fruits with sugar syrup - Peaches - Apricots - Plums - Bananas - Dried fruits

Oils and Fats

What to eat	What to avoid
- Macadamia nuts oil - Extra virgin olive oil - Butter - Ghee (clarified butter) - Flaxseeds oil - Walnut oil - Avocado oil - Almond oil	- Italian olive oil - Coconut oil - Soybean oil - Corn oil - Rapeseed oil - Cottonseed oil - Canola oil

Condiments

What to eat	What to avoid
- All spices (sugar-free) - Mayonnaise (sugar-free) - Aioli (sugar-free) - Pesto (sugar-free) - Guacamole (sugar-free) - Tomato paste (sugar-free) - Ranch dip (sugar-free) - Hollandaise sauce (sugar-free) - Vinegar (sugar-free)	- Ketchup - Molasses - Mustard - Sauerkraut - Seasoning mixes (containing salt) - Soy and teriyaki sauce

Grain products

What to eat	Enjoy occasionally	What to avoid
- Brown rice - Amaranth - Oatmeal - Quinoa - Millet - Whole grain bread - Buckwheat - Rye	- Barley - Corn - Bulgur	- White bread - White rice - Cereals - White-flour tortillas - Pasta

Beverages

What to eat	Enjoy occasionally	What to avoid
- Black/white coffee - Sparkling water - Iced water	- Light beer - Unsweetened tea	- Fruit punch - Fruit drinks - Fruit juice drinks - Energy drinks - Coffee with sugar and full-fat cream - Sweetened tea - Regular sodas - Regula beer - Sugar-sweetened drinks

Sweets

What to eat	Enjoy occasionally	What to avoid
- Stevia - Splenda - Truvia	- Monk Fruit - Tagatose	- Any types of artificial sugar (if it is not diabetic friendly) - White sugar - Brown sugar - Honey - Agave syrup - Maple syrup

What to Eat & Avoid | 9

BREAKFAST RECIPES

Breakfast Recipes

Chicken and Mushrooms Muffins

Servings: 4 | **Prep time:** 10 minutes
Cooking time: 7 minutes

Ingredients:

- 1 cup ground chicken
- 4 teaspoons almond flour
- 1 egg, beaten
- ½ teaspoon salt
- ½ cup cremini mushrooms, chopped
- ½ teaspoon ground black pepper
- 1 teaspoon olive oil
- ½ teaspoon chili flakes

Directions:

1. Combine ground chicken with almond flour, egg, salt, mushrooms, ground black pepper, olive oil, and chili flakes.
2. When it reaches the homogenous texture of the mass, transfer it to the silicone muffin molds.
3. Put the molds in the air fryer basket.
4. Cook the chicken muffins for 7 minutes at 400F.
5. Cool the cooked muffins to room temperature, then remove them from the muffin molds.

Nutrition value/serving: calories 107, fat 4.7, fiber 0.3, carbs 3.3, protein 11.8

Paprika Meatballs

Servings: 6 | **Prep time:** 10 minutes
Cooking time: 10 minutes

Ingredients:

- 1 cup ground beef
- 1 ½ cups ground chicken
- 1 ground paprika
- 1 tablespoon almond flour
- 1 teaspoon dried dill
- Cooking spray

Directions:

1. In the mixing bowl, combine ground beef, ground chicken, ground paprika, almond flour, and dried dill.
2. When the mixture reaches a homogenous texture, form the meatballs from it. Use the meatball scooper or make the meatballs with the help of your fingertips.
3. Spray the air fryer basket with the cooking spray from inside.
4. Arrange the meatballs in the air fryer basket.
5. Cook the meatballs for 10 minutes at 390F.

Nutrition value/serving: calories 112, fat 5.3, fiber 0.1, carbs 1.2, protein 14.7

Carrot Tots

Servings: 2 | **Prep time:** 15 minutes
Cooking time: 10 minutes

Ingredients:

- 4 carrots, peeled
- 1 teaspoon ground paprika
- ½ teaspoon salt
- ½ teaspoon turmeric
- 1 tablespoon almond meal
- 1 cup water, for cooking
- Cooking spray

Directions:

1. Pour water into the pan and bring it to a boil.
2. Add carrots, cover the pan with the lid, and boil them for 10 minutes or until the carrots are tender.
3. Drain the water and mash the vegetables with the help of the potato masher.
4. Add salt, ground paprika, turmeric, and almond meal.
5. Mix everything until homogenous.
6. Make the medium tots with the help of your fingertips.
7. Spray the air fryer basket with cooking spray and place the carrot tots inside.
8. Bake the tots at 395F for 5 minutes on each side.

Nutrition value/serving: calories 23, fat 1.6, fiber 0.9, carbs 1.9, protein 0.8

Parsley Meatballs

Servings: 4 | **Prep time:** 10 minutes
Cooking time: 13 minutes

Ingredients:

- 1 teaspoon Italian seasonings
- ¼ cup shallot, diced
- 1 teaspoon olive oil
- 1 cup ground pork
- 1 tablespoon fresh parsley, chopped
- ¼ teaspoon salt
- 1 egg, beaten
- 1 tablespoon almond flour

- Cooking spray

Directions:
1. Pour olive oil into the skillet and preheat it.
2. Add shallot and cook it until it is translucent.
3. Combine shallot, Italian seasonings, ground pork, parsley, salt, and egg.
4. Mix everything with a spoon.
5. Form the medium size meatballs from the mixture and sprinkle them gently with almond flour.
6. Coat the air fryer basket with cooking spray and place the meatballs inside.
7. Cook the meatballs for 10 minutes at 365F.
8. Flip the meatballs on another side and cook them for 3 additional minutes.

Nutrition value/serving: calories 275, fat 18.7, fiber 0.2, carbs 3.3, protein 21

Cottage Cheese Eggs
Servings: 5 | **Prep time:** 7 minutes
Cooking time: 5 minutes

Ingredients:
- 5 eggs, beaten
- ¼ teaspoon ground black pepper
- ½ teaspoon salt
- 1 tablespoon cottage cheese
- 1 teaspoon coconut butter

Directions:
1. Place the coconut butter in the air fryer cooking pan.
2. Insert it in the air fryer basket and preheat it to 365F.
3. When the coconut butter is melted, add beaten eggs, ground black pepper, salt, and cottage cheese, then whisk everything.
4. Cook the eggs for 3 minutes.
5. Open the air fryer and scramble the eggs with the fork.
6. Cook the scrambled eggs for 3 additional minutes.
7. You can extend the Cooking time if you prefer firm scrambled eggs.

Nutrition value/serving: calories 79, fat 5.8, fiber 0, carbs 0.6, protein 5.7

Spinach Pie
Servings: 6 | **Prep time:** 10 minutes
Cooking time: 20 minutes

Ingredients:
- 10 Phyllo sheets
- 2 cups spinach
- ½ cup Mozzarella, shredded
- 2 eggs, beaten
- ¼ cup coconut milk
- 1 teaspoon salt
- Cooking spray

Directions:
1. Combine coconut milk with beaten eggs, then add salt.
2. Coat the air fryer baking pan with cooking spray and place 5 Phyllo sheets inside. Flatten them if needed.
3. Chop the spinach and mix it with Mozzarella.
4. Top the Phyllo sheets with half of the spinach mixture and spread it evenly.
5. Cover the spinach mixture with 2 more Phyllo sheets and brush the surface with egg mixture.
6. Top everything with the remaining spinach mixture and cover with 3 more Phyllo sheets.
7. Brush the pie with the remaining egg mixture and transfer it to the air fryer basket.
8. Bake the pie for 20 minutes at 365F.
9. Allow the cooked pie to cool down and remove it from the cooking pan.
10. Slice it into the servings.

Nutrition value/serving: calories 203, fat 6.6, fiber 1.8, carbs 26.1, protein 8.2

Cod Balls
Servings: 2 | **Prep time:** 10 minutes
Cooking time: 10 minutes

Ingredients:
- ½ teaspoon mustard
- 6 oz cod fillet, diced
- 1 egg yolk
- ¼ teaspoon salt
- ¼ teaspoon ground cumin
- 2 teaspoons almond flour

Directions:

1. Combine all ingredients in the bowl.
2. With the help of the fingertips form the the balls from the mixture.
3. Place the cod balls in the air fryer basket.
4. Cook the balls at 375F for 5 minutes on each side.
5. The cooked fish balls will have a light brown color.

Nutrition value/serving: calories 151, fat 7.9, fiber 0.2, carbs 2.0, protein 18.4

Stuffed Tortillas

Servings: 4 | **Prep time:** 10 minutes
Cooking time: 10 minutes

Ingredients:

- 8 corn tortillas
- 1 cup Mozzarella, shredded
- 1/3 cup corn kernels, cooked
- Cooking spray

Directions:

1. Spray the air fryer baking pan with cooking spray.
2. Place 1 corn tortilla inside the baking pan and insert the pan into the air fryer.
3. Sprinkle the corn tortilla with Mozzarella and corn kernels.
4. Cover everything with the second corn tortilla.
5. Cook the quesadillas for 2 minutes on each side at 400F.
6. Repeat the same steps with all remaining corn tortillas.

Nutrition value/serving: calories 136, fat 2.8, fiber 3.4, carbs 24.1, protein 5.2

Fried Feta

Servings: 6 | **Prep time:** 10 minutes
Cooking time: 15 minutes

Ingredients:

- 1-pound block of low-fat Feta cheese
- 4 teaspoons Erythritol
- 4 teaspoons olive oil
- ½ teaspoon chili flakes
- ½ teaspoon dried dill

Directions:

1. Cut the Feta cheese block into 6 pieces and place them in the non-stick baking pan.
2. Put the pan in the air fryer.
3. Sprinkle the cheese with Erythritol, chili flakes, dried dill, and olive oil.
4. Brush the liquid with the silicone brush.
5. Cook the meal for 15 minutes at 365F.
6. Remove the cooked meal from the air fryer.
7. Use the silicone brush to spread the oily mixture on the surface of the meal and transfer it to the serving plates.

Nutrition value/serving: calories 258, fat 19.3, fiber 0, carbs 6.6, protein 13.5

Carrot Rolls

Servings: 4 | **Prep time:** 10 minutes
Cooking time: 15 minutes

Ingredients:

- 4 spring roll wrappers
- 7 oz shrimp, peeled
- ¼ teaspoon ground cumin
- 1 carrot, peeled
- 1 bell pepper, trimmed
- 1 tablespoon olive oil
- ¼ teaspoon salt
- 1 tablespoon fresh dill, chopped

Directions:

1. Cut the carrot and bell pepper into the wedges.
2. Put vegetable wedges in the hot non-stick skillet.
3. Roast them for 3 minutes over medium heat, stirring occasionally.
4. Transfer roasted vegetables to the bowl.
5. Place peeled shrimp in the skillet and cook them for 3 minutes.
6. Add the shrimp to the bowl too and mix up all ingredients.
7. Sprinkle prepared mixture with ground cumin, salt, and fresh dill.
8. Place the mixture in the center of every spring roll wrap and roll them up.
9. Brush the spring rolls with olive oil and arrange them in the air fryer basket.
10. Cook the spring rolls for 3 minutes on each side at 385F.
11. The cooked carrot spring rolls will be light brown in color.

Nutrition value/serving: calories 207, fat 5.9, fiber 1.4, carbs 23.1, protein 14.9

Oregano Eggs

Servings: 4 | **Prep time:** 5 minutes
Cooking time: 6 minutes

Ingredients:

- 4 eggs
- 1 teaspoon dried oregano
- 2 teaspoons olive oil
- ¾ teaspoon salt

Directions:

1. Preheat the air fryer to 365F.
2. Brush the ramekins with olive oil.
3. In a shallow bowl, combine oregano and salt.
4. Crack an egg in each ramekin and top them with the oregano mixture.
5. Arrange the ramekins with eggs in the air fryer basket and bake them for 6 minutes or until the eggs are firm.

Nutrition value/serving: calories 81, fat 6.4, fiber 0.2, carbs 0.6, protein 5.6

Coconut Pancakes

Servings: 6 | **Prep time:** 10 minutes
Cooking time: 4 minutes

Ingredients:

- 1 ½ cups coconut flour
- 1 teaspoon baking soda
- ½ teaspoon apple cider vinegar
- 1 teaspoon vanilla extract
- 1 tablespoon ground cinnamon
- 1 tablespoon Erythritol
- 1 tablespoon olive oil
- 1 cup coconut milk
- Cooking spray

Directions:

1. In the mixing bowl, combine coconut flour, baking soda, apple cider vinegar, vanilla extract, ground cinnamon, olive oil, Erythritol, and coconut milk to make the pancake batter. Whisk the mixture until smooth and homogeneous.
2. Coat the ramekins with cooking spray from the inside.
3. Fill each ramekin with pancake batter halfway and sprinkle with Erythritol.
4. Arrange the ramekins in the air fryer basket.
5. Cook the pancakes for 4 minutes at 395F.
6. The pancakes are cooked when they are light brown on a surface.

Nutrition value/serving: calories 167, fat 2.3, fiber 1.4, carbs 31.1, protein 4.6

Turmeric Eggs

Servings: 2 | **Prep time:** 10 minutes
Cooking time: 10 minutes

Ingredients:

- 2 teaspoons olive oil
- ¼ teaspoon ground black pepper
- ¾ teaspoon ground turmeric
- 4 eggs, cracked
- 1 large bell pepper

Directions:

1. Cut the bell pepper in half and remove the seeds from the inside.
2. Pour the olive oil inside every bell pepper half.
3. Crack 2 eggs in each bell pepper half and top them with ground black pepper and turmeric.
4. Arrange the pepper boats in the air fryer basket.
5. Cook the peppers for 10 minutes at 365F or until the eggs are firm.

Nutrition value/serving: calories 182, fat 12.8, fiber 1.1, carbs 5.9, protein 11.8

Vanilla Toasts

Servings: 4 | **Prep time:** 10 minutes
Cooking time: 6 minutes

Ingredients:

- 4 whole-grain bread slices
- 2 eggs, beaten
- ¼ cup coconut milk
- 1 teaspoon coconut flour
- 1 teaspoon vanilla extract
- 1 tablespoon Erythritol
- Cooking spray

Directions:

1. Whisk together beaten eggs and coconut milk.
2. Add coconut flour, vanilla extract, and stir until smooth.
3. Dip each bread slice in the egg mixture and leave them for 5 minutes or until the bread soaks the milk mixture.
4. Preheat the air fryer to 375F.
5. Spray the air fryer baking pan with cooking

spray.
6. Place the dipped bread slices in the baking pan and insert them into the air fryer.
7. Cook the toast for 3 minutes.
8. Then flip them to another side.
9. The cooked toasts will have a golden-brown crust.
10. Sprinkle the cooked hot toast with the Erythritol on both sides.

Nutrition value/serving: calories 76, fat 2.8, fiber 0.5, carbs 8.9, protein 4

Garlic Eggs

Servings: 2 | **Prep time:** 10 minutes
Cooking time: 11 minutes

Ingredients:

- 4 eggs
- ¾ teaspoon ground garlic
- 1 cup ice water, for peeling

Directions:

1. Place the eggs in the air fryer basket.
2. Cook the eggs for 11 minutes at 270F.
3. When the eggs are cooked, place them in the ice water immediately and leave for 5 minutes.
4. Peel the eggs and cut them into halves.
5. Sprinkle every egg half with ground garlic.

Nutrition value/serving: calories 126, fat 8.8, fiber 0, carbs 0.7, protein 11.1

Apricot Fritters

Servings: 4 | **Prep time:** 10 minutes
Cooking time: 10 minutes

Ingredients:

- 1 cup coconut flour
- 2 apricots, pitted, grated
- 1 egg, beaten
- 2 tablespoons Greek yogurt
- 1 tablespoon Erythritol
- ½ teaspoon vanilla extract
- 1 teaspoon avocado oil

Directions:

1. In the bowl, combine coconut flour, grated apricots, egg, Greek yogurt, Erythritol, and vanilla extract to make the fritters dough.
2. Mix everything with the a spoon until smooth.
3. Line the bottom of the air fryer basket with parchment and brush it with avocado oil.
4. With the help of the spoon make fritters and place them in the air fryer basket.
5. Cook the fritters at 375F for 5 minutes on each side.

Nutrition value/serving: calories 203, fat 3.3, fiber 6.4, carbs 40.7, protein 6

Kale Cakes

Servings: 6 | **Prep time:** 15 minutes
Cooking time: 9 minutes

Ingredients:

- 1-pound kale, chopped
- 1 egg, beaten
- 2 tablespoons Plain yogurt
- 1 teaspoon salt
- ½ cup coconut flour
- ¼ teaspoon ground cumin
- 1 teaspoon olive oil

Directions:

1. Mix chopped kale with salt and let it sit for 10 minutes or until it releases the juice.
2. Add egg, Plain yogurt, coconut flour, and ground cumin.
3. Stir the fritter mixture well.
4. Brush the air fryer baking pan with olive oil.
5. With the help of the spoon make the medium size fritters and place them in the baking pan.
6. Insert the baking pan into the preheated to 385F air fryer.
7. Cook the fritters for 5 minutes.
8. Flip them on another side and bake for 4 additional minutes.

Nutrition value/serving: calories 64, fat 1.7, fiber 0.6, carbs 9.2, protein 2.5

Thyme Muffins

Servings: 4 | **Prep time:** 15 minutes
Cooking time: 4 minutes

Ingredients:

- 1 egg, beaten
- 4 tablespoons rolled oats
- 1 cup sweet potato, boiled, mashed
- 1 tablespoon fresh parsley, chopped
- 1 teaspoon fresh dill, chopped
- 1/3 cup white onion, diced
- 1 teaspoon olive oil
- ½ teaspoon salt

- ¼ teaspoon dried thyme

Directions:
1. In the bowl combine egg, rolled oats, mashed sweet potato, parsley, dill, salt, and thyme to make the muffin dough. Stir the mixture until smooth.
2. Preheat the skillet and add oil.
3. Add diced onion and cook it until light brown.
4. Add the cooked onion to the sweet potato mixture. Stit it until smooth.
5. Transfer the muffin mixture to the silicone muffin mold and flatten the surface.
6. Place the muffins in the air fryer basket.
7. Bake the muffins for 4 minutes at 400F.
8. Let the muffins cool down to room temperature and remove them from the molds.

Nutrition value/serving: calories 65, fat 2.6, fiber 1.2, carbs 7.2, protein 2.6

Beef Rolls

Servings: 3 | **Prep time:** 10 minutes
Cooking time: 15 minutes

Ingredients:
- 3 egg roll wraps
- 1 oz chives, chopped
- 7 oz extra-lean ground beef
- ¼ teaspoon minced garlic
- ¾ teaspoon ground ginger
- ¼ teaspoon salt
- 1 teaspoon olive oil

Directions:
1. Preheat olive oil in the skillet.
2. Add ground beef, chives, minced garlic, ground ginger, and salt and stir the mixture.
3. Roast it for 10 minutes over medium heat, stirring occasionally.
4. Place the ground beef mixture in the middle of each egg roll wrap.
5. Roll up the egg roll and transfer them to the air fryer basket.
6. Bake the egg rolls for 3 minutes at 400 F.
7. Flip them on another side and bake for an additional minute.

Nutrition value/serving: calories 252, fat 9.7, fiber 1.6, carbs 19.1, protein 20.7

Avocado Cups

Servings: 4 | **Prep time:** 10 minutes
Cooking time: 6 minutes

Ingredients:
- 1 avocado, peeled, pitted, and chopped
- 1 cup broccoli, shredded
- 4 eggs, beaten
- 4 tablespoons coconut cream
- 1 red onion, diced
- 1 teaspoon olive oil
- 1 tablespoon wheat flour, whole grain
- ½ teaspoon ground black pepper
- ¼ teaspoon salt

Directions:
1. Combine all the ingredients together.
2. Pour the mixture into the silicone muffin molds.
3. Insert the molds in the air fryer.
4. Cook the vegetable cups for 6 minutes at 400F (including time for air fryer preheating).
5. Chill the cooked vegetable cups to room temperature, then remove them from the molds.

Nutrition value/serving: calories 117, fat 6.2, fiber 2.1, carbs 9.3, protein 7.3

Cheese Sandwich

Servings: 2 | **Prep time:** 15 minutes
Cooking time: 14 minutes

Ingredients:
- 4 slices of multigrain bread
- 2 oz cottage cheese, low-fat
- 2 oz Mozzarella, shredded
- 1 egg, beaten
- ¼ cup coconut milk
- 1 teaspoon olive oil

Directions:
1. Make the sandwiches by placing Mozzarella and cottage cheese on 2 bread slices. Then cover it with the remaining bread slices.
2. In the mixing bowl, whisk together coconut milk and beaten egg.
3. Dip every sandwich in the egg mixture and leave for 3 minutes.
4. Prepare 2 foil squares and brush them with olive oil from the inside.
5. Transfer the dipped sandwiches to the foil and wrap them.

6. Put the wrapped sandwiches in the air fryer and cook for 10 minutes at 360F.
7. Remove the sandwiches from the air fryer and discard the foil.
8. Return the sandwiches to the air fryer basket and bake for 2 more minutes on each side at 400F.

Nutrition value/serving: calories 354, fat 17, fiber 4.6, carbs 27.1, protein 23

Chicken Chimichangas

Servings: 4 | **Prep time:** 10 minutes
Cooking time: 10 minutes

Ingredients:
- 4 corn tortillas
- 7 oz chicken breast, skinless, boneless, boiled
- 3 oz white beans, canned, drained
- 1 teaspoon taco seasoning
- 1 tablespoon avocado oil
- 4 oz Mozzarella cheese, shredded, low-fat
- 1 tablespoon green chilies, minced
- 1 teaspoon olive oil

Directions:
1. Preheat avocado oil in the skillet.
2. Shred the boiled chicken breast with the help of the fork and transfer it to the skillet.
3. Sprinkle the shredded chicken with taco seasoning and green chiles. Stir well and cook for 3 minutes over medium heat.
4. Mash the white beans with potato masher.
5. Add mashed beans to the chicken and stir well.
6. Cook the ingredients for 2 additional minutes.
7. Place the mixture in the center of each corn tortilla and spread evenly.
8. Top the mixture with shredded cheese and fold up the edges.
9. Roll the tortillas to get the medium size pockets.
10. Brush the tortilla pockets with olive oil and arrange them in the air fryer basket.
11. Cook chimichangas at 400F for 2 minutes on each side.

Nutrition value/serving: calories 278, fat 8.7, fiber 4.9, carbs 25.7, protein 24.7

Asparagus Omelette

Servings: 4 | **Prep time:** 10 minutes
Cooking time: 15 minutes

Ingredients:
- 1 cup asparagus, chopped
- 1 tablespoon olive oil
- 2 tablespoons plain yogurt
- 6 eggs, beaten
- 1 teaspoon salt
- ½ teaspoon chili flakes
- 1 tablespoon chives, chopped
- Cooking spray

Directions:
1. Preheat a skillet and pour olive oil inside.
2. Add chopped asparagus.
3. Roast the asparagus for 5 minutes over medium heat, stirring occasionally.
4. In the mixing bowl, combine plain yogurt, beaten eggs, salt, chili flakes, and chives.
5. Add cooked and chilled asparagus to the egg mixture. Stir it gently.
6. Coat the air fryer baking pan with cooking pray from inside and pour the egg mixture. Flatten everything.
7. Insert the baking pan into the air fryer basket.
8. Cook the omelet for 5 minutes at 400F or until it is firm.

Nutrition value/serving: calories 137, fat 10.7, fiber 0.1, carbs 16, protein 9

Nutmeg Eggs

Servings: 3 | **Prep time:** 15 minutes
Cooking time: 6 minutes

Ingredients:
- 1 cup fresh spinach
- 3 eggs
- 3 teaspoons olive oil
- ½ teaspoon salt
- ¾ teaspoon ground nutmeg

Directions:
1. Place the spinach, salt and ground nutmeg in the blender.
2. Blend the mass until soft and smooth.
3. Crack the eggs in the bowl and add blended spinach. Stir thoroughly.
4. Grease the ramekins with the olive oil and pour

the spinach-egg mixture inside.
5. Insert the ramekins into the air fryer basket.
6. Bake the eggs for 6 minutes at 350F.

Nutrition value/serving: calories 135, fat 11, fiber 0.4, carbs 1.3, protein 8.3

Potato Sticks

Servings: 2 | **Prep time:** 20 minutes
Cooking time: 5 minutes

Ingredients:

- 1 egg, beaten
- 3 tablespoons coconut flour
- 1 cup sweet potato, peeled mashed
- 1 teaspoon rolled oats
- ½ teaspoon salt

Directions:

1. In the mixing bowl, combine rolled oats, sweet potato, and salt.
2. When you get a homogenous mixture form the small balls from it and press them with your palms to get the shape of sticks.
3. Place the potato "sticks" in the freezer for 15 minutes.
4. Remove the "sticks" from the freezer and dip in the beaten egg.
5. Coat the potato "sticks" in the coconut flour mixture and transfer them to the air fryer basket.
6. Roast the meal for 3 minutes at 400F. Then flip them and cook for 2 additional minutes.
7. The cooked potato "sticks" will be golden brown.

Nutrition value/serving: calories 152, fat 7.1, fiber 1.5, carbs 14.1, protein 8.1

Cilantro Casserole

Servings: 5 | **Prep time:** 10 minutes
Cooking time: 20 minutes

Ingredients:

- 1 cup fresh cilantro, chopped
- 5 eggs, beaten
- ½ white onion, diced
- 1 teaspoon ground paprika
- 1 tablespoon olive oil
- ¼ cup coconut milk

Directions:

1. In the mixing bowl, combine cilantro with beaten eggs, onion, ground paprika, and coconut milk.
2. Brush the silicone mold with olive oil.
3. Pour the mixture into the silicone mold.
4. Transfer it to the air fryer basket and cook the meal at 365F for 20 minutes.

Nutrition value/serving: calories 265, fat 19.1, fiber 1.4, carbs 12.9, protein 10.3

Cherry Tomato Pizzas

Servings: 4 | **Prep time:** 10 minutes
Cooking time: 3 minutes

Ingredients:

- 2 bagels, whole-grain, diabetic-friendly
- 1 teaspoon sesame seeds
- 2 cherry tomatoes, crushed
- 1 teaspoon dried thyme

Directions:

1. Cut the bagels lengthwise into 2 halves.
2. Spread each bagel half with crushed tomatoes.
3. Sprinkle the bagels with sesame seeds, and dried thyme.
4. Put the bagel pizzas in the air fryer basket and close the lid.
5. Cook the bagel pizzas for 3 minutes at 400F.

Nutrition value/serving: calories 160, fat 2.5, fiber 1.3, carbs 27.2, protein 7.5

Fish Quesadillas

Servings: 4 | **Prep time:** 15 minutes
Cooking time: 10 minutes

Ingredients:

- 6 Phyllo sheets
- 6 oz tilapia fillet, boiled, chopped
- ¼ teaspoon minced garlic
- 1/3 teaspoon salt
- 1 tablespoon fresh parsley, chopped
- 1 tablespoon cottage cheese
- 1 teaspoon olive oil

Directions:

1. Brush the air fryer baking pan with half a teaspoon of olive oil and place 3 Phyllo sheets inside. Flatten them if needed.
2. In the mixing bowl, combine tilapia, salt, and parsley in the mixing bowl.
3. Mix cottage cheese with minced garlic.

4. Spread prepared Phyllo sheets with a cottage cheese mixture.
5. Add mashed tilapia mixture and flatten it gently.
6. Cover the tilapia with remaining Phyllo sheets and brush with remaining olive oil.
7. Cook the quesadilla for 6 minutes at 385F.
8. Quesadilla is cooked when it has a golden crust.
9. Cool the meal for 10 minutes, then cut into 4 servings.

Nutrition value/serving: calories 241, fat 9.2, fiber 1.5, carbs 23.2, protein 16

Gyros

Servings: 2 | **Prep time:** 10 minutes
Cooking time: 4 minutes

Ingredients:

- 2 corn tortillas
- 2 scrambled eggs
- 1 cucumber, chopped
- 1 bell pepper, sliced
- 1 teaspoon olive oil

Directions:

1. Place scrambled eggs in the center of each flour tortilla.
2. Add chopped cucumber and bell pepper.
3. Fold the sides of the tortillas and roll them up.
4. Brush the gyros with olive oil.
5. Transfer the gyros to the air fryer basket.
6. Bake the gyros at 365F for 2 minutes on each side.

Nutrition value/serving: calories 593, fat 39.9, fiber 1.5, carbs 23.1, protein 34.3

Coriander Chicken Fillets

Servings: 2 | **Prep time:** 10 minutes
Cooking time: 10 minutes

Ingredients:

- 6 oz chicken fillets, cut into halves
- 1 teaspoon ground coriander
- ½ teaspoon salt
- ½ teaspoon ground turmeric
- 2 teaspoons olive oil
- 1 teaspoon lemon juice

Directions:

1. Beat the chicken fillets gently with the kitchen hammer.
2. Sprinkle the chicken with ground coriander, salt, and ground turmeric.
3. Combine olive oil with lemon juice.
4. Brush the chicken fillets with the oil mixture on both sides and transfer them to the air fryer basket.
5. Roast the chicken fillets for 10 minutes at 375F.

Nutrition value/serving: calories 208, fat 11.3, fiber 0.3, carbs 0.8, protein 24.9

Beef and Eggs

Servings: 3 | **Prep time:** 15 minutes
Cooking time: 15 minutes

Ingredients:

- 1 ½ cups ground beef
- 1 yellow onion, diced
- ½ teaspoon dried basil
- 1 teaspoon salt
- ½ teaspoon sage
- ½ teaspoon ground cumin
- ½ teaspoon dried cilantro
- 3 eggs, boiled, peeled
- 2 eggs, beaten
- 1/3 cup almond flour

Directions:

1. In the mixing bowl, combine ground beef, diced onion, basil, salt, sage, ground cumin, and dried cilantro.
2. From 3 balls from the meat mixture and press them gently to get a flat cake.
3. Place the boiled egg in the center of every meat cake.
4. Roll them up into the meatballs.
5. Coat the meatballs in the almond flour, then dip them in the beaten egg.
6. Transfer the prepared meatballs to the air fryer basket.
7. Bake the meal at 375F for 15 minutes.
8. The cooked eggs will have a golden brown crust.

Nutrition value/serving: calories 355, fat 16.9, fiber 1.8, carbs 24.1, protein 26.2

Chicken Pockets

Servings: 4 | **Prep time:** 15 minutes
Cooking time: 12 minutes

Ingredients:

- 1 cup almond flour
- 3 tablespoons Greek yogurt
- ¾ teaspoon salt
- 5 oz chicken fillet, boiled, sliced
- 1 egg, beaten
- 1 teaspoon olive oil

Directions:

1. Make the dough: combine almond flour with yogurt and salt. Knead the dough until soft and non-sticky.
2. Cut it into 4 parts and roll them out into a rectangular shape.
3. Place sliced chicken on each dough rectangular and roll them up.
4. Seal the ends of the dough with the help of the fork.
5. Brush the pockets with egg and olive oil.
6. Place the pockets in the air fryer baking pan and transfer them to the air fryer. Close the lid.
7. Cook the hot pockets for 10 minutes at 375F.
8. Flip the meal into another side and bake for 2 additional minutes.
9. The cooked chicken pockets will be golden brown.

Nutrition value/serving: calories 318, fat 15, fiber 1.3, carbs 26.5, protein 18.1

Meat Roll

Servings: 2 | **Prep time:** 10 minutes
Cooking time: 4 minutes

Ingredients:

- 2 large egg roll wrappers
- 5 oz corned beef, cooked
- 1 teaspoon Greek yogurt
- Cooking spray

Directions:

1. Shred the corned beef with the fork and transfer it to the bowl.
2. Add Greek yogurt, and mix well.
3. Place the mixture in the center of every egg roll wrapper and fold them up in the shape of pockets.
4. Coat the egg rolls with cooking spray and arrange them in the preheated to 375F air fryer basket.
5. Roast the rolls for 2 minutes on each side at 375F.

Nutrition value/serving: calories 226, fat 10.2, fiber 1.8, carbs 19.6, protein 13.9

Avocado Canoes

Servings: 2 | **Prep time:** 8 minutes
Cooking time: 8 minutes

Ingredients:

- 1 avocado, pitted, halved
- 2 eggs
- ¼ teaspoon ground paprika
- ½ teaspoon avocado oil
- 1 teaspoon scallions, chopped

Directions:

1. Crack the eggs into the avocado holes and sprinkle them with paprika and scallions.
2. Brush the avocado with avocado oil and insert it in the air fryer basket.
3. Roast avocados for 8 minutes at 360F.

Nutrition value/serving: calories 278, fat 25.1, fiber 6.8, carbs 9.1, protein 7.5

Wrapped Chicken

Servings: 4 | **Prep time:** 15 minutes
Cooking time: 5 minutes

Ingredients:

- 1-pound chicken fillet, boiled, shredded
- 7 oz sourdough, diabetic-friendly
- 2 teaspoon tomato sauce, sugar-free

Directions:

1. Roll out the sourdough and cut it into 4 triangles.
2. Place chicken on each triangle. Roll the triangles.
3. Skew rolled chicken wraps onto the bamboo skewers and transfer them to the air fryer basket.
4. Bake the wrapped chicken for 5 minutes at 385F or until they are light brown.
5. Sprinkle cooked-wrapped chicken with tomato sauce.

Nutrition value/serving: calories 281, fat 13.5, fiber 1.6, carbs 25.1, protein 12.7

Broccoli and Sauce Bites

Servings: 2 | **Prep time:** 10 minutes
Cooking time: 20 minutes

Ingredients:

- 1 cup broccoli florets
- 2 tablespoon BBQ sauce, sugar-free
- 2 tablespoons coconut flour
- ½ teaspoon ground black pepper
- Cooking spray

Directions:

1. Combine broccoli florets with BBQ Sauce, and ground black pepper.
2. Sprinkle the vegetables with coconut flour and shake well.
3. Transfer the broccoli florets to the air fryer basket and spray them with cooking spray.
4. Roast the broccoli florets at 330F for 20 minutes.
5. Shake the broccoli florets after 10 minutes of cooking.

Nutrition value/serving: calories 69, fat 0.5, fiber 1.7, carbs 14.4, protein 1.9

Wonton Crab Meat

Servings: 4 | **Prep time:** 15 minutes
Cooking time: 6 minutes

Ingredients:

- 4 wonton wrappers
- 9 oz crab meat, canned, drained
- 1 tablespoon cottage cheese
- ¼ teaspoon ground garlic
- 1 teaspoon olive oil

Directions:

1. In the mixing bowl, combine crab meat with cottage cheese and ground garlic until everything is homogeneous.
2. Fill the wonton wrappers with crab mixture and secure the edges carefully.
3. Brush the wonton wraps with olive oil and transfer them to the air fryer basket.
4. Roast the meal for 6 minutes at 385F or until they are golden and crispy.

Nutrition value/serving: calories 171, fat 3.7, fiber 0.6, carbs 19.9, protein 11.3

Oregano and Chicken Meatballs

Servings: 6 | **Prep time:** 15 minutes
Cooking time: 10 minutes

Ingredients:

- 2 tablespoons sriracha sauce
- 1 chili pepper, minced
- 2 cups ground chicken
- 1 egg, beaten
- 1 teaspoon salt
- 1 tablespoon dried oregano
- 2 tablespoons water
- 1/3 cup coconut flour
- 1 teaspoon minced garlic
- ½ teaspoon ground nutmeg
- Cooking spray

Directions:

1. In the mixing bowl, combine all the ingredients except cooking spray and sriracha sauce.
2. Form the meatballs from the meat mixture and place them in the air fryer basket. Coat them with cooking spray.
3. Roast chicken meatballs for 7 minutes at 385F.
4. Flip the meatballs and brush them with sriracha sauce.
5. Cook the meatballs for 3 minutes more.

Nutrition value/serving: calories 136, fat 6.7, fiber 0.7, carbs 6.9, protein 10.6

Crushed Eggs

Servings: 4 | **Prep time:** 5 minutes
Cooking time: 5 minutes

Ingredients:

- 4 eggs, beaten
- 1 zucchini, grated
- 2 tablespoons water
- 1 teaspoon olive oil
- ¼ teaspoon chili flakes
- 1/3 teaspoon salt

Directions:

1. Pour olive oil into the air fryer baking pan.
2. Add grated zucchini, salt, and chili flakes. Stir well.
3. Place the baking pan in the air fryer.
4. Roast it for 2 minutes at 400F.
5. Stir well, then add water and beaten eggs.
6. Scramble the eggs for 1 minute and roast for 3

minutes at 400F.
7. Stir the egg mixture again and transfer it to the serving plates.

Nutrition value/serving: calories 87, fat 5.7, fiber 0.8, carbs 3.3, protein 6.2

Paprika Beef Bars

Servings: 3 | **Prep time:** 8 minutes
Cooking time: 14 minutes

Ingredients:
- 1 cup ground beef
- 1 teaspoon olive oil
- ½ tablespoon tomato paste
- ½ teaspoon chili powder
- ½ teaspoon ground paprika
- ½ teaspoon salt

Directions:
1. Line the air fryer baking pan with parchment.
2. Combine ground beef with olive oil, chili powder, ground paprika, and salt.
3. Transfer the mixture to the parchment and flatten it in one layer.
4. Place the baking pan in the air fryer.
5. Roast the ground beef for 10 minutes at 365F.
6. Cut roasted ground beef into bars and spread it with tomato paste.
7. Bake it for 4 minutes more at 375F.
8. Cool the cooked bars a little and transfer them to the serving plates.

Nutrition value/serving: calories 136, fat 8.9, fiber 0.2, carbs 1.7, protein 11.8

SIDE DISHES

Side Dishes

Sweet Potato Fries

Servings: 4 | **Prep time:** 10 minutes
Cooking time: 9 minutes

Ingredients:

- 2 sweet potatoes
- 1 teaspoon ground paprika
- 1 teaspoon salt
- 1 tablespoon olive oil

Directions:

1. Clean sweet potatoes well and cut them into the French fries shape.
2. Sprinkle the fries with olive oil well and place them in the air fryer in one layer.
3. Cook them for 9 minutes at 395F. Flip the fries on another side after 6 minutes of cooking.
4. Mix together salt and ground paprika.
5. Transfer the cooked side dish to the plate and sprinkle with the prepared spice mixture.

Nutrition value/serving: calories 97, fat 3.5, fiber 2, carbs 16.4, protein 1

Curry Fries

Servings: 2 | **Prep time:** 10 minutes
Cooking time: 8 minutes

Ingredients:

- 2 Russet potatoes
- 1 teaspoon curry powder
- 1 teaspoon avocado oil

Directions:

1. Peel Russet potatoes and make the curls from them with the spiralizer.
2. Sprinkle the vegetables with curry powder and avocado oil.
3. Transfer the curly potatoes to the air fryer and close the lid.
4. Cook them for 8 minutes at 395F. Shake the fries after 4 minutes of cooking.
5. Curly fries are cooked when they are golden brown.

Nutrition value/serving: calories 172, fat 2.7, fiber 5.4, carbs 29, protein 3.7

Dill Potato

Servings: 4 | **Prep time:** 10 minutes
Cooking time: 24 minutes

Ingredients:

- 1 ½ cups potato wedges
- 1 tablespoon dried dill
- 1 tablespoon olive oil
- 1 teaspoon salt
- 1 teaspoon dried parsley

Directions:

1. In the mixing bowl, combine potato wedges with dried parsley, olive oil, salt, and dried dill. Stir well.
2. Preheat the air fryer to 400F.
3. Arrange the potato wedges in the air fryer in one layer.
4. Cook the potato wedges for 4 minutes on each side.
5. Repeat the same steps with the remaining uncooked potatoes.

Nutrition value/serving: calories 77, fat 4.3, fiber 0.8, carbs 8.6, protein 1

Nutmeg Mushrooms

Servings: 2 | **Prep time:** 8 minutes
Cooking time: 13 minutes

Ingredients:

- 1 cup mushrooms, halved
- ½ teaspoon salt
- 1 teaspoon ground nutmeg
- ½ lemon
- 2 tablespoons olive oil
- 1 tablespoon fresh dill, chopped

Directions:

1. Place the mushrooms in the mixing bowl.
2. Sprinkle them with salt and ground nutmeg.
3. Add olive oil and mix the mushrooms well.
4. Place the mushrooms in the air fryer.
5. Cook them at 385F for 13 minutes. Stir the vegetables every 4 minutes.
6. Transfer the cooked mushrooms to the serving bowl and sprinkle with lemon juice and fresh dill. Stir gently.

Nutrition value/serving: calories 141, fat 14.2, fiber 1.2, carb 3.2, protein 1.6

Cauliflower Mix

Servings: 5 | **Prep time:** 10 minutes
Cooking time: 15 minutes

Ingredients:

- 1 red potato, sliced
- 1 cup cauliflower, chopped
- 1 cup red bell pepper, roughly chopped
- 1 zucchini, sliced
- 1 teaspoon garlic powder
- 3 tablespoons olive oil
- ¾ cup soy sauce
- 1 teaspoon chili flakes
- ½ teaspoon ground paprika
- ½ teaspoon minced garlic
- 1 oz Mozzarella, shredded

Directions:

1. In a small bowl, combine olive oil with minced garlic, ground paprika, chili flakes, soy sauce, olive oil, and garlic powder. Whisk the mixture gently.
2. Place all the vegetables in the big mixing bowl.
3. Pour the oil mixture over the vegetables and stir them well.
4. Transfer the mixture to the air fryer.
5. Cook the vegetables for 15 minutes at 390F.
6. Shake them gently every 5 minutes.
7. Transfer the cooked meal to the serving plates and top with shredded Mozzarella.

Nutrition value/serving: calories 176, fat 9.9, fiber 3.3, carbs 17.4, protein 7

Turmeric Eggplant Fries

Servings: 2 | **Prep time:** 20 minutes
Cooking time: 16 minutes

Ingredients:

- 1 large eggplant, trimmed
- 1 teaspoon salt
- 1 teaspoon ground turmeric
- 1 teaspoon olive oil

Directions:

1. Cut the eggplants into the French fries shape and sprinkle with salt, and let the vegetables sit for 10 minutes.
2. Dry the eggplant fries with a paper towel and sprinkle with olive oil. Shake gently.
3. Transfer the fries to the air fryer in one layer.
4. Cook them at 400F for 4 minutes on each side.
5. Repeat the same steps with the remaining eggplant fries.
6. Transfer the cooked eggplants to the plate and sprinkle them with turmeric.

Nutrition value/serving: calories 80, fat 2.7, fiber 8.2, carbs 14.2, protein 2.4

Beef Wraps

Servings: 6 | **Prep time:** 15 minutes
Cooking time: 11 minutes

Ingredients:

- 8 oz pizza dough, diabetic, sugar-free
- 8 oz beef loin, boiled, shredded
- Cooking spray

Directions:

1. Roll out the pizza dough.
2. Cut it into 6 squares.
3. Place the shredded beef in the center of each dough square.
4. Fold the squares gently to form the triangles.
5. Secure the edges of triangles with the fork.
6. Coat the air fryer basket with the cooking spray from inside.
7. Arrange the triangles in the air fryer basket.
8. Cook the beef wraps for 11 minutes at 400F or until they are light brown.

Nutrition value/serving: calories 321, fat 21.6, fiber 2, carbs 17.2, protein 12.1

Hot Cakes

Servings: 6 | **Prep time:** 10 minutes
Cooking time: 12 minutes

Ingredients:

- 1 cup cauliflower, shredded
- ½ teaspoon chili powder
- ½ teaspoon salt
- 1 teaspoon dried parsley
- 1 tablespoon almond flour
- 1 egg, beaten
- Cooking spray

Directions:

1. In the mixing bowl, combine shredded cauliflower with salt, dried parsley, egg, almond flour, and chili powder until everything is homogenous.
2. Form 6 balls from the cauliflower mixture and

press them gently into the shape of round cakes.
3. Coat the air fryer basket with cooking spray from the inside.
4. Arrange the cauliflower cakes in the air fryer in one layer
5. Cook the cauliflower cakes at 400F for 6 minutes on each side or until they are golden brown.

Nutrition value/serving: calories 41, fat 2.3, fiber 0.6, carbs 2.1, protein 2.6

Broccoli Wings

Servings: 5 | **Prep time:** 15 minutes
Cooking time: 16 minutes

Ingredients:

- 1 cup broccoli florets
- 1 tablespoon ground paprika
- ½ teaspoon salt
- ¾ cup Erythritol
- 1 teaspoon onion powder
- ½ teaspoon chili flakes
- ½ teaspoon ground black pepper
- 2 eggs, beaten
- 2 tablespoons coconut flour
- ¼ cup coconut milk
- Cooking spray

Directions:

1. In the mixing bowl, combine ground paprika, salt, Erythritol, onion powder, chili flakes, ground black pepper, and coconut flour.
2. Add eggs and coconut milk and stir the mixture until homogenous.
3. Place the broccoli florets in the paprika batter and coat them well.
4. Then place the broccoli florets in the air fryer basket and sprinkle them with the cooking spray.
5. Cook the broccoli wings at 375F for 8 minutes on each side.

Nutrition value/serving: calories 197, fat 2.3, fiber 1, carbs 42.4, protein 3.5

Chili Wedges

Servings: 3 | **Prep time:** 10 minutes
Cooking time: 8 minutes

Ingredients:

- 2 Russet potatoes, washed
- 1 teaspoon salt
- 1 tablespoon chili flakes
- 1 tablespoon canola oil
- Cooking spray

Directions:

1. Cut the potatoes into the medium size wedges and sprinkle them with salt. Mix up well.
2. Coat the air fryer with the cooking spray from inside and place potato wedges.
3. Cook the potatoes at 385F for 4 minutes on each side.
4. The potato wedges are cooked when they are light brown.
5. Transfer the cooked vegetables to the plate and sprinkle with canola oil and chili flakes.

Nutrition value/serving: calories 139, fat 4.3, fiber 4.3, carbs 23.6, protein 2.8

Cinnamon Apples

Servings: 4 | **Prep time:** 10 minutes
Cooking time: 2 minutes

Ingredients:

- 2 Granny Smith apples, peeled
- 1 tablespoon olive oil
- 1 tablespoon ground cinnamon

Directions:

1. In the mixing bowl, combine olive oil and ground cinnamon. Stir gently.
2. Slice the apples into pieces and add them to the bowl.
3. Coat the apples into the cinnamon mixture and transfer them to the air fryer.
4. Cook the apples for 2 minutes at 365F.
5. Gently stir the cooked apples and transfer them to the serving plates.

Nutrition value/serving: calories 90, fat 3.3, fiber 2.9, carbs 16.9, protein 0.4

Thyme Asparagus

Servings: 2 | **Prep time:** 10 minutes
Cooking time: 8 minutes

Ingredients:

- 4 oz asparagus
- ¼ teaspoon salt
- 1 egg, beaten
- ¼ teaspoon dried thyme
- ¼ cup coconut flour

- Cooking spray

Directions:
1. Trim the asparagus if needed.
2. In the mixing bowl, combine egg, salt, and dried thyme.
3. Dip the asparagus in the egg mixture.
4. Coat asparagus in the coconut flour.
5. Arrange the asparagus in the air fryer basket and spray it with cooking spray.
6. Cook the vegetables at 395F for 4 minutes on each side.

Nutrition value/serving: calories 97, fat 3, fiber 1.9, carbs 12.3, protein 5.9

Parsley Kebabs

Servings: 2 | **Prep time:** 10 minutes
Cooking time: 3 minutes

Ingredients:
- 2 bell peppers
- 1 tablespoon lime juice
- 1 teaspoon canola oil
- ½ teaspoon dried parsley
- Cooking spray

Directions:
1. Trim the bell peppers and remove the seeds.
2. Cut the peppers into halves, then cut the pepper halves into squares.
3. Skew the pepper squares onto the wooden skewers and coat them with cooking spray.
4. Place the pepper skewers (kebabs) in the air fryer.
5. Cook them at 400F for 3 minutes.
6. In a shallow bowl, combine dried parsley, canola oil, and lime juice.
7. Transfer the cooked pepper kebabs to the plate and sprinkle with the oil mixture.

Nutrition value/serving: calories 62, fat 2.7, fiber 1.6, carbs 9.8, protein 1.3

Ginger Squash

Servings: 6 | **Prep time:** 15 minutes
Cooking time: 11 minutes

Ingredients:
- 1-pound yellow squash
- ½ teaspoon ground ginger
- 1 tablespoon sesame oil

Directions:
1. Chop the squash into small pieces and sprinkle them with ground ginger.
2. Mix well and sprinkle the vegetables with sesame oil. Stir well again.
3. Transfer the squash pieces to the air fryer basket.
4. Cook the meal for 11 minutes at 400F. Stir the squash every 2 minutes.

Nutrition value/serving: calories 33, fat 2.4, fiber 0.9, carbs 2.6, protein 0.9

Black Pepper Brussels Sprout Halves

Servings: 2 | **Prep time:** 15 minutes
Cooking time: 10 minutes

Ingredients:
- 1 cup Brussels sprouts
- 1 teaspoon ground black pepper
- 1 tablespoon avocado oil
- 1 tablespoon balsamic vinegar
- 1 teaspoon soy sauce, sugar-free

Directions:
1. Trim Brussels sprouts and cut them into halves. Transfer the vegetables to the mixing bowl.
2. Add ground black pepper, avocado oil, balsamic vinegar, and soy sauce. Mix the ingredients well and transfer them to the air fryer basket. Close the lid.
3. Cook the meal for 10 minutes at 400F. Stir the vegetables every 3 minutes.
4. When the Brussels sprouts are cooked, transfer them to the serving plates.

Nutrition value/serving: calories 132, fat 10.2, fiber 1.8, carbs 5.8, protein 6.5

Soy Sauce Rice

Servings: 8 | **Prep time:** 10 minutes
Cooking time: 5 minutes

Ingredients:
- 2 cups white rice, cooked
- 1 teaspoon soy sauce, sugar-free
- 1 teaspoon salt
- 1 teaspoon dried parsley
- 2 tablespoons olive oil
- 1 teaspoon ground black pepper

Directions:
1. Place the cooked rice in the baking pan.

2. Add olive oil, salt, ground black pepper, and parsley. Mix well.
3. Place the baking pan in the air fryer. Cover the pan with foil and secure the edges.
4. Cook the rice for 5 minutes at 400F. Stir the rice after 3 minutes.
5. Remove the foil from the rice.
6. Add soy sauce to the rice and stir well.

Nutrition value/serving: calories 199, fat 3.5, fiber 0.7, carbs 37.4, protein 3.4

Chili Eggplant Coins

Servings: 4 | **Prep time:** 15 minutes
Cooking time: 10 minutes

Ingredients:
- 2 tablespoons lemon juice
- 1 garlic clove, diced
- 2 tablespoons olive oil
- 1 teaspoon salt
- 1 teaspoon chili flakes
- 2 eggplants, sliced
- 1 tablespoon fresh dill, chopped
- Cooking spray

Directions:
1. Place the eggplants in the mixing bowl. Add salt and mix well.
2. Leave the eggplants sit for 10 minutes until it releases the juice.
3. Transfer the vegetables to the air fryer basket and sprinkle them with cooking spray.
4. Cook the eggplants for 10 minutes at 350F, stirring occasionally.
5. Transfer them to the salad bowl.
6. Add diced garlic, chili flakes, dill, and olive oil.
7. Sprinkle the eggplants with lemon juice and mix well.
8. Leave the eggplants for 10 minutes to rest in the fridge.

Nutrition value/serving: calories 132, fat 7.5, fiber 9.7, carbs 16.5, protein 2.8

Radish Hash

Servings: 2 | **Prep time:** 10 minutes
Cooking time: 10 minutes

Ingredients:
- 1 cup radish, sliced
- ½ cup white onion, sliced
- ½ teaspoon salt
- ½ teaspoon ground black pepper
- 3 tablespoons avocado oil

Directions:
1. In the mixing bowl, combine radish, white onion, salt, and ground black pepper.
2. Mix well and transfer it to the air fryer basket.
3. Sprinkle the mixture with avocado oil.
4. Cook the meal at 360F for 10 minutes, stirring occasionally to avoid burning.

Nutrition value/serving: calories 202, fat 21.1, fiber 1.7, carbs 5, protein 0.8

Garlic Green Beans

Servings: 4 | **Prep time:** 10 minutes
Cooking time: 7 minutes

Ingredients:
- 1-pound green beans
- 1 garlic clove, minced
- 1 teaspoon ground black pepper
- ½ teaspoon salt
- 1 teaspoon dried dill
- 3 tablespoons avocado oil

Directions:
1. In the mixing bowl, combine ground black pepper, garlic, salt, and dried dill.
2. Add avocado oil and stir gently.
3. Brush the green beans with the oil mixture or just sprinkle them with it, then transfer them to the air fryer basket.
4. Flatten the green beans and cook them at 395F for 7 minutes, stirring occasionally.

Nutrition value/serving: calories 59, fat 1.6, fiber 4.8, carbs 11.1, protein 2.6

Chili Turnips

Servings: 3 | **Prep time:** 10 minutes
Cooking time: 15 minutes

Ingredients:
- 1 ½ cups turnip, peeled, cut into the chunks
- 1 teaspoon dried dill
- ½ teaspoon salt
- ½ teaspoon chili flakes
- 1 tablespoon olive oil

Directions:
1. Place the turnip in the bowl and sprinkle with

dried dill, salt, chili flakes, and olive oil. Mix well.
2. Transfer the ingredients to the air fryer basket and flatten them.
3. Cook the turnip for 15 minutes at 400F, stirring occasionally to avoid burning.

Nutrition value/serving: calories 60, fat 4.6, fiber 1.3, carbs 4.6, protein 0.7

Avocado Patties

Servings: 3 | **Prep time:** 15 minutes
Cooking time: 8 minutes

Ingredients:
- 2 oz white beans, canned, drained
- 2 oz avocado, peeled, pitted
- 1 teaspoon dried parsley
- 1 egg, beaten
- ½ teaspoon ground paprika
- 1 tablespoon almond flour
- 1 teaspoon olive oil

Directions:
1. Place the beans and avocado in the blender.
2. Blend the ingredients until smooth.
3. Add dried parsley, egg, ground paprika, and almond flour.
4. Pulse the mixture until everything is homogenous (approximately 10 seconds).
5. Form the patties from the mixture and place them in the air fryer basket.
6. Brush them with olive oil.
7. Cook the patties for 4 minutes on each side at 400F.

Nutrition value/serving: calories 150, fat 7, fiber 4.4, carbs 16.1, protein 7

Garlic Tempeh

Servings: 3 | **Prep time:** 10 minutes
Cooking time: 8 minutes

Ingredients:
- 6 oz tempeh
- 3 tablespoons soy sauce, sugar-free
- ¼ teaspoon liquid smoke
- ½ teaspoon sesame oil
- ½ teaspoon Erythritol
- 1 garlic clove, peeled, minced
- ¾ teaspoon ground paprika
- 1 tablespoon water

Directions:
1. Slice the tempeh thinly.
2. In the mixing bowl, combine soy sauce, liquid smoke, sesame oil, Erythritol, garlic, and ground paprika.
3. Place the tempeh in the marinade and leave for 10 minutes to marinade.
4. Remove the tempeh from the marinade and transfer it to the air fryer.
5. Sprinkle it with a quarter of the amount of the remaining marinade.
6. Cook the tempeh for 5 minutes at 400F, then flip it on another side and cook for 3 minutes more.

Nutrition value/serving: calories 127, fat 6.9, fiber 0.2, carbs 7.2, protein 11.6

Garlic Cauliflower

Servings: 4 | **Prep time:** 8 minutes
Cooking time: 22 minutes

Ingredients:
- 1-pound cauliflower, chopped
- 1 garlic clove, minced
- ½ teaspoon red pepper powder
- 1 tablespoon olive oil
- ½ teaspoon dried dill

Directions:
1. In the mixing bowl, combine cauliflower, minced garlic, red pepper powder, and dried dill. Stir the mixture well.
2. Transfer it to the air fryer and close the lid.
3. Cook the cauliflower at 395F for 22 minutes. Stir it every 5 minutes.

Nutrition value/serving: calories 112, fat 7, fiber 1.1, carbs 7, protein 5.5

Dill Broccoli Rice

Servings: 2 | **Prep time:** 10 minutes
Cooking time: 6 minutes

Ingredients:
- ½ cup broccoli, shredded
- 1 tablespoon olive oil
- ½ teaspoon salt
- ½ teaspoon dried dill
- ½ teaspoon ground turmeric

Directions:
1. In the mixing bowl, combine broccoli with salt,

dried dill, and ground turmeric.
2. Add olive oil and stir well.
3. Transfer the mixture to the air fryer.
4. Cook the broccoli rice for 6 minutes at 400F. Stir the "rice" every 2 minutes to avoid burning.

Nutrition value/serving: calories 60, fat 5.9, fiber 0.8, carbs 1.8, protein 0.7

Paprika Cauliflower Rice

Servings: 4 | **Prep time:** 10 minutes
Cooking time: 5 minutes

Ingredients:

- ½ cup fresh parsley, chopped
- 1 tablespoon olive oil
- ½ teaspoon avocado oil
- ½ teaspoon paprika
- 9 oz cauliflower, shredded
- ½ teaspoon chili flakes
- ½ teaspoon sage
- ¾ teaspoon dried oregano
- 1 garlic clove, diced

Directions:

1. In the mixing bowl, combine shredded cauliflower, chili flakes, sage, dried oregano, and diced garlic.
2. Add olive and avocado oils. Stir the mixture until homogenous.
3. Transfer the cauliflower rice to the baking pan and flatten it well.
4. Place the baking pan in the air fryer.
5. Cook the cauliflower rice for 5 minutes at 400F. Stir the side dish well after 4 minutes of cooking. Add Cooking time if cauliflower rice is not crunchy enough.
6. Combine hot cauliflower rice with fresh parsley, and transfer the meal to the serving plates.

Nutrition value/serving: calories 63, fat 4.2, fiber 2.1, carbs 4.9, protein 2

Zucchini Burgers

Servings: 2 | **Prep time:** 10 minutes
Cooking time: 20 minutes

Ingredients:

- 1 zucchini, peeled
- 1 egg, beaten
- 1 teaspoon chives
- ½ teaspoon salt
- 1 tablespoon almond flour
- 1 sweet potato, boiled, peeled
- Cooking spray

Directions:

1. Blend the zucchini with sweet potato until smooth.
2. Add egg, chives, salt, and almond flour.
3. Pulse the mixture for 10 seconds or until homogenous.
4. Coat the air fryer basket with cooking spray.
5. Make the small burgers from the zucchini mixture and transfer them to the air fryer.
6. Spray the burgers with cooking spray.
7. Cook them at 355F for 10 minutes on each side.

Nutrition value/serving: calories 150, fat 4.9, fiber 6.7, carbs 21.1, protein 7.1

Parsley Zucchini

Servings: 2 | **Prep time:** 10 minutes
Cooking time: 25 minutes

Ingredients:

- 1 zucchini, trimmed, sliced
- ¼ teaspoon salt
- ½ teaspoon white pepper
- 1 teaspoon fresh parsley, chopped
- 1 tablespoon olive oil

Directions:

1. In the big bowl, combine sliced zucchini, salt, white pepper, and olive oil. Mix well and transfer the vegetables to the air fryer basket. Flatten them gently.
2. Cook zucchini for 25 minutes at 355F. Flip the zucchini on another side every 5 minutes.
3. Transfer the cooked zucchini to the plates and top with fresh parsley.

Nutrition value/serving: calories 80, fat 70.2, fiber 1.3, carbs 3.9, protein 1.4

Appetizer Garlic Bulbs

Servings: 8 | **Prep time:** 10 minutes
Cooking time: 21 minutes

Ingredients:

- 1-pound garlic bulb, unpeeled
- 1 teaspoon dried thyme
- 2 tablespoons avocado oil
- 1/3 teaspoon salt

Directions:

1. Peel the garlic bulbs and place them on the foil.
2. Sprinkle the vegetables with dried thyme, avocado oil, and salt.
3. Wrap the garlic in the foil and transfer it to the air fryer.
4. Cook the meal at 400F for 21 minutes.
5. Discard the foil from the garlic and squeeze the bulb to get all the garlic flesh.
6. Stir it gently and transfer it to the small serving bowl.

Nutrition value/serving: calories 31, fat 3.5, fiber 0.1, carbs 0.5, protein 0

Cilantro and Chickpea Fritters

Servings: 2 | **Prep time:** 10 minutes
Cooking time: 6 minutes

Ingredients:

- ½ cup chickpeas, canned, rinsed
- 2 tablespoons rolled oats
- ¼ teaspoon salt
- ¼ teaspoon chili flakes
- ¼ cup fresh cilantro, chopped
- 1 egg, beaten
- 1 teaspoon ground black pepper
- Cooking spray

Directions:

1. Blend the chickpeas with cilantro until you get a soft and smooth mass.
2. Transfer blended mixture to the bowl and add rolled oats, salt, chili flakes, egg, and ground black pepper. Stir well.
3. Form the balls from the mixture and press them into the shape of the fritters.
4. Coat the air fryer basket with the cooking spray.
5. Place the fritters in the air fryer.
6. Cook them at 400F for 3 minutes on each side.
7. Cook for a couple more minutes, if you want to get a crunchy crust.

Nutrition value/serving: calories 238, fat 5.7, fiber 9.7, carbs 35.1, protein 13.3

Buffalo Style Broccoli

Servings: 4 | **Prep time:** 10 minutes
Cooking time: 14 minutes

Ingredients:

- 2 cups broccoli florets
- ½ cup Buffalo sauce
- 1 tablespoon olive oil

Directions:

1. In the mixing bowl, combine broccoli florets and Buffalo sauce.
2. Sprinkle the air fryer basket with olive oil.
3. Place the broccoli florets in the air fryer and flatten them gently.
4. Cook the meal for 14 minutes at 365F, stirring occasionally to avoid burning.

Nutrition value/serving: calories 22, fat 0.1, fiber 2, carbs 4.2, protein 1

Garlic Asparagus

Servings: 4 | **Prep time:** 15 minutes
Cooking time: 15 minutes

Ingredients:

- 10 oz asparagus
- ½ teaspoon salt
- 1 teaspoon ground garlic
- 1 teaspoon olive oil

Directions:

1. Trim the asparagus if needed and sprinkle it with salt, ground garlic, and olive oil.
2. Transfer the asparagus to the air fryer basket.
3. Cook the meal at 350F for 15 minutes. Turn the asparagus on another side after 10 minutes of cooking.

Nutrition value/serving: calories 101, fat 7.2, fiber 1.5, carbs 3, protein 6.8

Fragrant Buns

Servings: 4 | **Prep time:** 5 minutes
Cooking time: 4 minutes

Ingredients:

- 4 whole-grain buns
- 1 egg, beaten
- 1 tablespoon coconut cream
- ½ teaspoon ground cinnamon
- Cooking spray

Directions:

1. Mix together the egg with coconut cream and ground cinnamon.
2. Dip the buns in the egg mixture.
3. Transfer them to the air fryer.
4. Spray the meal with cooking spray.

5. Cook the buns for 4 minutes at 395F.

Nutrition value/serving: calories 260, fat 4.1, fiber 2.4, carbs 46.2, protein 9.4

Thyme Spaghetti Squash

Servings: 5 | **Prep time:** 10 minutes
Cooking time: 30 minutes

Ingredients:

- 1-pound spaghetti squash, halved
- ½ teaspoon dried thyme
- 2 tablespoons olive oil

Directions:

1. Sprinkle the spaghetti squash halves with thyme and olive oil.
2. Place the vegetable halves in the air fryer.
3. Cook them for 30 minutes at 365F.
4. Transfer the cooked squash to the plate and shred it with the fork.

Nutrition value/serving: calories 76, fat 6.1, fiber 0, carbs 6.3, protein 0.6

Garlic and Carrot Puree

Servings: 4 | **Prep time:** 10 minutes
Cooking time: 6 minutes

Ingredients:

- 2 carrots, peeled
- 1 tablespoon coconut milk
- 1 garlic clove, peeled, minced
- 1 teaspoon avocado oil

Directions:

1. Place the carrots and minced garlic in the air fryer and sprinkle with avocado oil.
2. Cook the vegetables for 6 minutes at 400F.
3. Remove the cooked carrots and garlic from the air fryer and blend them until smooth.
4. Transfer the carrot puree to the bowl, add coconut milk, and stir well.

Nutrition value/serving: calories 38, fat 3, fiber 0.9, carbs 3, protein 0.3

Sage Shredded Cabbage

Servings: 2 | **Prep time:** 10 minutes
Cooking time: 10 minutes

Ingredients:

- 1 cup white cabbage, shredded
- 1 tablespoon olive oil
- ½ teaspoon salt
- 1 tablespoon dried sage

Directions:

1. Place shredded cabbage in the air fryer and sprinkle it with salt, dried sage, and olive oil.
2. Stir the ingredient gently.
3. Cook the cabbage at 375F for 10 minutes, stirring occasionally.

Nutrition value/serving: calories 61, fat 5.9, fiber 0.9, carbs 2.2, protein 0.6

Lemon Purple Cabbage

Servings: 6 | **Prep time:** 10 minutes
Cooking time: 12 minutes

Ingredients:

- 12 oz purple cabbage
- 2 tablespoons olive oil
- 1 tablespoon lemon juice
- ¼ teaspoon ground black pepper

Directions:

1. Cut the purple cabbage into small steaks.
2. In the shallow bowl, combine olive oil, lemon juice, and ground black pepper.
3. Brush each cabbage steak with the oil mixture and transfer it to the air fryer.
4. Cook the cabbage at 400F for 6 minutes on each side.

Nutrition value/serving: calories 69, fat 4.8, fiber 1.6, carbs 7.1, protein 0.9

Coriander Portobello Caps

Servings: 2 | **Prep time:** 10 minutes
Cooking time: 5 minutes

Ingredients:

- 2 Portobello caps
- 2 teaspoons cottage cheese
- ¼ teaspoon salt
- ¼ teaspoon ground coriander
- 1 tablespoon sesame oil

Directions:

1. Place Portobello caps in the air fryer.
2. In the mixing bowl, combine cottage cheese, salt, ground coriander, and sesame oil.
3. Fill each Portobello cap with cottage cheese mixture.
4. Cook the side dish for 5 minutes at 400F.

Nutrition value/serving: calories 83, fat 9.5, fiber 1, carbs 3.1, protein 0

Cumin Brussels Sprouts

Servings: 4 | Prep time: 20 minutes
Cooking time: 9 minutes

Ingredients:

- 2 cups Brussels sprouts
- 1 teaspoon balsamic vinegar
- 1 teaspoon avocado oil
- ½ teaspoon ground cumin

Directions:

1. Place Brussels sprouts in the air fryer.
2. Sprinkle the vegetables with avocado oil, ground cumin, and balsamic vinegar.
3. Stir the Brussels sprouts gently.
4. Cook the meal for 9 minutes at 375F, stirring occasionally.

Nutrition value/serving: calories 146, fat 10.2, fiber 1.7, carbs 2.3, protein 9.4

Ginger Plantains

Servings: 4 | Prep time: 5 minutes
Cooking time: 9 minutes

Ingredients:

- 3 plantains
- 2 tablespoons olive oil
- ¼ teaspoon ground ginger

Directions:

1. Peel and slice the plantains.
2. Combine olive oil with ground ginger.
3. Brush the sliced plantains with oil mixture on both sides and transfer them to the air fryer basket.
4. Cook the meal for 9 minutes at 355F. Flip the plantains on another side during cooking.

Nutrition value/serving: calories 224, fat 7.3, fiber 3.2, carbs 42.9, protein 1.8

Turmeric Cabbage Wedges

Servings: 4 | Prep time: 10 minutes
Cooking time: 8 minutes

Ingredients:

- 1-pound cabbage, cut into the wedges
- 4 tablespoons olive oil
- 3 tablespoons balsamic vinegar
- 1 teaspoon ground turmeric
- ¼ teaspoon ground paprika

Directions:

1. In a shallow bowl, combine olive oil, balsamic vinegar, ground turmeric, and paprika.
2. Brush each cabbage wedge with the oil mixture and transfer it to the air fryer in one layer.
3. Cook the cabbage wedges for 5 minutes at 365F.
4. Flip the vegetables to another side and cook for 3 minutes more.

Nutrition value/serving: calories 151, fat 14.1, fiber 2.9, carbs 6.7, protein 1.5

FISH & SEAFOOD

Fish and Seafood

Garlic Shrimps

Servings: 4 | **Prep time:** 25 minutes
Cooking time: 5 minutes

Ingredients:

- 9 oz shrimp, peeled
- 1 teaspoon minced garlic
- ½ teaspoon salt
- 2 tablespoons olive oil
- 3 tablespoons lemon juice

Directions:

1. In the mixing bowl, combine minced garlic, salt, olive oil, and lemon juice to make the marinade.
2. Place shrimp in the big bowl and pour marinade over them. Mix well and leave it for 20 minutes to marinate.
3. Preheat the air fryer to 400F.
4. Place the marinated shrimps in the air fryer and flatten them gently.
5. Cook the meal for 5 minutes at 400F or until they are light red (pink).

Nutrition value/serving: calories 202, fat 8.3, fiber 0.3, carbs 16, protein 15.7

Cod Patties

Servings: 3 | **Prep time:** 10 minutes
Cooking time: 7 minutes

Ingredients:

- 5 oz cod fillet, boiled
- 1 teaspoon onion powder
- 1 teaspoon dried thyme
- ½ teaspoon ground cumin
- ¼ teaspoon salt
- ¼ teaspoon ground black pepper
- 2 tablespoons rolled oats
- 1 teaspoon olive oil

Directions:

1. Place the cod in the bowl and shred it with the fork.
2. Add onion powder, dried thyme, ground cumin, salt, ground black pepper, and rolled oats.
3. Stir the cod mixture until homogenous.
4. Form the patties from the fish mixture.
5. Brush the air fryer basket with olive oil from the inside and place the patties.
6. Cook the patties at 400F for 4 minutes. Then flip them on another side and cook for 3 minutes more or until the patties are golden brown.

Nutrition value/serving: calories 96, fat 4.8, fiber 0.9, carbs 4.2, protein 9.9

Coriander Lobster Tails

Servings: 2 | **Prep time:** 10 minutes
Cooking time: 5 minutes

Ingredients:

- 2 lobster tails
- ¼ teaspoon ground coriander
- 1/3 teaspoon salt
- 1 tablespoon olive oil
- ½ teaspoon lemon juice

Directions:

1. In the mixing bowl, churn together softened olive oil, lemon juice, salt, and ground coriander.
2. Spread the lobster tails with the coriander mixture generously and place them in the air fryer basket.
3. Cook lobster tails at 375F for 5 minutes.

Nutrition value/serving: calories 102, fat 6, fiber 0.2, carbs 0.6, protein 0.2

Paprika Crab Cakes

Servings: 4 | **Prep time:** 10 minutes
Cooking time: 15 minutes

Ingredients:

- 1 teaspoon chili powder
- ½ teaspoon salt
- ½ teaspoon ground black pepper
- 1 teaspoon ground paprika
- ½ teaspoon dried parsley
- 2 tablespoons almond flour
- 1 teaspoon lemon juice
- 12 oz crab meat
- Cooking spray

Directions:

1. In the mixing bowl, combine chili powder, salt, ground black pepper, ground paprika, dried parsley, almond flour, lemon juice, and crab meat.
2. Stir the mixture until homogenous.
3. Make the small balls (cakes) from the crab

mixture and arrange them in the air fryer.
4. Spray them with cooking spray.
5. Cook the crab cakes for 15 minutes at 365F.

Nutrition value/serving: calories 101, fat 1.9, fiber 0.8, carbs 6.7, protein 11.5

Italian Seasoning Shrimps

Servings: 2 | **Prep time:** 15 minutes
Cooking time: 6 minutes

Ingredients:
- 6 oz shrimp, peeled
- 1 tablespoon Italian seasoning
- 1 teaspoon olive oil

Directions:
1. Mix the shrimp with Italian seasoning.
2. Place the shrimp in the air fryer basket and sprinkle with olive oil.
3. Cook the shrimp for 6 minutes at 395F or until they are light pink.

Nutrition value/serving: calories 188, fat 4.3, fiber 1.4, carbs 11.9, protein 25.2

Garlic Mussels

Servings: 2 | **Prep time:** 10 minutes
Cooking time: 4 minutes

Ingredients:
- 2 tablespoons olive oil
- ½ teaspoon minced garlic
- ¼ teaspoon ground paprika
- ½ teaspoon basil
- ½ teaspoon dried thyme
- 13 oz mussels
- ½ cup water

Directions:
1. Pour water into the baking pan and insert it into the air fryer basket.
2. Add mussels and sprinkle them with garlic, ground paprika, basil, and thyme.
3. Cook mussels for 4 minutes at 400F.
4. Drain the cooked mussels and transfer them to the serving bowl.
5. Sprinkle the hot mussels with olive oil.

Nutrition value/serving: calories 263, fat 15.7, fiber 0.3, carbs 7.4, protein 22.2

Coriander Tilapia Fillets

Servings: 6 | **Prep time:** 10 minutes
Cooking time: 10 minutes

Ingredients:
- 2-pound tilapia fillets
- 1 teaspoon olive oil
- ½ teaspoon ground coriander
- 1 teaspoon ground paprika
- ½ teaspoon salt

Directions:
1. In the mixing bowl, combine salt, ground paprika, and ground coriander.
2. Cut tilapia fillets into the servings and mix them with the coriander mixture.
3. Brush the air fryer basket with olive oil from the inside.
4. Transfer the tilapia fillets to the air fryer.
5. Cook the fish for 8 minutes at 400F.
6. Gently flip the fish to another side and cook for 2 minutes more.

Nutrition value/serving: calories 161, fat 4.2, fiber 0.6, carbs 1.1, protein 29.4

Lime Salmon

Servings: 2 | **Prep time:** 10 minutes
Cooking time: 8 minutes

Ingredients:
- 10 oz salmon fillet
- 1 tablespoon olive oil
- 1 teaspoon ranch seasonings
- 1 tablespoon lime juice
- ½ teaspoon dried parsley

Directions:
1. In the mixing bowl, combine ranch seasonings and dried parsley.
2. Rub the salmon fillet with spices and brush with olive oil.
3. Transfer the fish to the air fryer and cook for 8 minutes at 390F.
4. When the fish is cooked, cut it into 2 parts and sprinkle it with lime juice.

Nutrition value/serving: calories 256, fat 15.8, fiber 0, carbs 0.2, protein 27.6

Chili Cod en Papilote

Servings: 2 | **Prep time:** 10 minutes
Cooking time: 17 minutes

Ingredients:
- 8 oz cod (2 fillets)
- 2 bell peppers, sliced, julienned
- 1 teaspoon chili powder
- 2 teaspoons olive oil
- ½ teaspoon salt
- ½ teaspoon ground paprika
- 1 red onion, sliced
- 2 teaspoons lemon juice

Directions:
1. Cut the parchment paper into 2 squares and fold them into boats.
2. Place bell peppers on the parchment.
3. Add sliced onion.
4. In the mixing bowl, combine chili powder, olive oil, salt, ground paprika, and lemon juice.
5. Brush the cod with oil mixture from each side and place over the vegetables on parchment.
6. Transfer the meal to the air fryer.
7. Cook the fish for 17 minutes at 365F.

Nutrition value/serving: calories 271, fat 10.1, fiber 4.6, carbs 18.3, protein 28.5

Spinach Cod

Servings: 4 | **Prep time:** 10 minutes
Cooking time: 15 minutes

Ingredients:
- 1 ½-pounds cod fillet
- 1 cup spinach
- 1 tablespoon lemon juice
- 1 teaspoon olive oil

Directions:
1. Blend spinach with lemon juice and olive oil until smooth.
2. Coat the cod fillet in the spinach mixture.
3. Wrap the fish in foil and place it in the air fryer.
4. Cook the fish for 15 minutes at 385F.
5. When the cod is cooked, remove it from the air fryer and discard the foil.
6. Cut the fish into servings.

Nutrition value/serving: calories 227, fat 10.2, fiber 0.3, carbs 1.3, protein 32.4

Coriander Tilapia Sticks

Servings: 4 | **Prep time:** 15 minutes
Cooking time: 6 minutes

Ingredients:
- 1-pound tilapia fillet
- ½ cup almond flour
- 2 tablespoons coconut milk
- ½ teaspoon ground coriander
- ½ teaspoon ground turmeric
- Cooking spray

Directions:
1. Cut the tilapia fillet into wedges (sticks).
2. Sprinkle the fish with ground coriander and turmeric.
3. Brush the fish with coconut milk.
4. In the mixing bowl almond flour.
5. Coat every fish stick in almond flour and transfer it to the air fryer.
6. Cook the tilapia sticks for 3 minutes on each side at 400F.

Nutrition value/serving: calories 206, fat 6, fiber 0.6, carbs 10.7, protein 27.7

Tender Mackerel

Servings: 4 | **Prep time:** 15 minutes
Cooking time: 9 minutes

Ingredients:
- 14 oz mackerel, fillet
- 1 teaspoon lemon juice
- 1 teaspoon ground paprika
- 1 tablespoon almond flour
- 1 teaspoon avocado oil
- ½ teaspoon salt

Directions:
1. In the mixing bowl, combine lemon juice, ground paprika, and salt.
2. Rub the fillet with the spice mixture well.
3. Coat the mackerel in the almond flour.
4. Sprinkle the fish with avocado oil and arrange it in the air fryer.
5. Cook it for 5 minutes at 385F.
6. Flip the fish to another side and cook it for 4 minutes more.

Nutrition value/serving: calories 303, fat 20.6, fiber 0.4, carbs 2.3, protein 25.8

Cumin Catfish

Servings: 2 | **Prep time:** 10 minutes
Cooking time: 10 minutes

Ingredients:

- 8 oz catfish fillet
- 1 teaspoon ground cumin
- ½ teaspoon salt
- ½ teaspoon dried dill
- ½ teaspoon olive oil

Directions:

1. Cut the catfish fillet into two servings.
2. Rub the fish fillets with salt, dried dill, and ground cumin.
3. Brush the air fryer basket with olive oil.
4. Place the catfish fillets in the air fryer.
5. Cook the fish for 5 minutes on each side at 395F.

Nutrition value/serving: calories 194, fat 10.2, fiber 0.6, carbs 6.4, protein 18.2

Chili Crab Bites

Servings: 2 | **Prep time:** 15 minutes
Cooking time: 10 minutes

Ingredients:

- 8 oz crab meat
- 2 tablespoons almond flour
- 1 egg, beaten
- 1 teaspoon chili powder
- 1 teaspoon dried oregano
- 1 teaspoon ground cumin
- 2 tablespoons lime juice
- 1 teaspoon olive oil

Directions:

1. Place the crab meat in the big bowl and churn it with the fork.
2. Add almond flour, chili powder, egg, lemon juice, dried oregano, and ground cumin. Stir well.
3. Form the medium "fingers" from the crab mixture and coat them in bread crumbs.
4. Transfer the fingers to the air fryer and sprinkle with olive oil.
5. Cook the crab fingers for 5 minutes on each side at 380F or until golden brown.

Nutrition value/serving: calories 191, fat 7.2, fiber 1.2, carbs 9.5, protein 18.2

Garlic Kampung Fish

Servings: 2 | **Prep time:** 20 minutes
Cooking time: 9 minutes

Ingredients:

- 8 oz kampung fish
- 1 tablespoon olive oil
- 1 teaspoon minced garlic
- ½ teaspoon ground black pepper
- ½ teaspoon salt
- 2 tablespoons lemon juice

Directions:

1. Rub the fish with minced garlic, ground black pepper, and salt.
2. Sprinkle it with lemon juice and olive oil. Leave the fish for 15 minutes to marinate.
3. Place the marinated fish in the air fryer.
4. Cook it for 4 minutes at 400F.
5. Flip the fish to another side and cook for 5 more minutes.

Nutrition value/serving: calories 255, fat 17.2, fiber 0.2, carbs 0.9, protein 22.6

Nutmeg Tilapia

Servings: 4 | **Prep time:** 25 minutes
Cooking time: 10 minutes

Ingredients:

- 12 oz tilapia, trimmed
- 1 lemon
- 1 teaspoon ground nutmeg
- 1 tablespoon olive oil
- 4 tablespoons water

Directions:

1. Make the diagonal cuts in the tilapia.
2. Rub the fish with ground nutmeg.
3. Squeeze the juice of a lemon over the tilapia and massage it.
4. Sprinkle the fish with olive oil and water.
5. Transfer the fish to the air fryer basket. Leave it for 10-15 minutes to marinate.
6. Cook the tilapia for 5 minutes on each side at 395F.

Nutrition value/serving: calories 118, fat 4.6, fiber 1.2, carbs 3.8, protein 16.5

Cumin Sea Bass

Servings: 2 | **Prep time:** 30 minutes
Cooking time: 8 minutes

Ingredients:

- 9 oz sea bass, trimmed
- ½ cup lemon juice
- ½ teaspoon salt
- ¼ teaspoon ground cumin
- 6 teaspoons olive oil
- 1/3 cup water

Directions:

1. In the mixing bowl, combine lemon juice, olive oil, salt, ground cumin, and water.
2. Roughly chop the sea bass roughly and place it in the lemon mixture. Mix gently and leave for 25 minutes to marinate.
3. Remove the fish from the marinade and transfer it to the air fryer basket.
4. Spray it with oil spray and cook at 400F for 4 minutes on each side.

Nutrition value/serving: calories 317, fat 17.3, fiber 1.5, carbs 7.1, protein 31.3

Cilantro Cod

Servings: 3 | **Prep time:** 35 minutes
Cooking time: 15 minutes

Ingredients:

- 13 oz cod fillet
- 1 tablespoon tomato paste
- 1 tablespoon dried cilantro
- 4 tablespoons olive oil
- ½ teaspoon salt
- 1 tablespoon soy sauce, sugar-free

Directions:

1. In the mixing bowl, combine soy sauce and tomato paste.
2. Add olive oil, cilantro, and stir the mixture until homogenous.
3. Rub the cod fillet with tomato sauce well and leave it for 30 minutes in the fridge to marinate.
4. Wrap the fish in the foil and put it in the air fryer.
5. Cook it for 15 minutes at 375F.

Nutrition value/serving: calories 272, fat 19.8, fiber 0.4, carbs 1.6, protein 22.5

Turmeric Calamari Rings

Servings: 2 | **Prep time:** 15 minutes
Cooking time: 8 minutes

Ingredients:

- 7 oz calamari, trimmed
- 1 teaspoon ground turmeric
- ½ teaspoon salt
- ½ cup almond flour
- 2 eggs, beaten
- 1 tablespoon olive oil

Directions:

1. Slice the calamari into rings.
2. Put them in the bowl and add eggs. Stir well.
3. In the separate bowl, mix together ground turmeric, salt, and almond flour.
4. Coat every calamari ring in the almond flour mixture.
5. Transfer the "rings" to the air fryer basket and sprinkle them with olive oil.
6. Cook them for 8 minutes at 360F. Stir the calamari rings after 4 minutes of cooking.

Nutrition value/serving: calories 363, fat 11.2, fiber 3.1, carbs 52.9, protein 13.1

Dill Squids

Servings: 4 | **Prep time:** 10 minutes
Cooking time: 20 minutes

Ingredients:

- 4 squid tubes, trimmed
- ½ yellow onion, diced
- 1 tablespoon tomato paste
- 1 teaspoon garlic clove, diced
- ½ cup of brown rice, cooked
- 1 tablespoon fresh dill, chopped
- 1 tablespoon olive oil

Directions:

1. In the mixing bowl, combine rice, onion, tomato paste, garlic clove, and parsley.
2. Fill the squid tubes with rice mixture and secure the edges with toothpicks.
3. Brush every squid tube with olive oil and transfer it to the air fryer.
4. Cook the meal at 365F for 10 minutes on each side.

Nutrition value/serving: calories 187, fat 5.1, fiber 1, carbs 21.4, protein 14.2

Chili Cod Fillets

Servings: 4 | **Prep time:** 35 minutes
Cooking time: 7 minutes

Ingredients:

- 1-pound cod fillet
- 1 teaspoon chili powder
- ½ teaspoon apple cider vinegar
- 1 tablespoon olive oil
- ½ teaspoon ground cumin
- ½ teaspoon fennel seeds

Directions:

1. In the bowl, combine apple cider vinegar, chili powder, olive oil, ground cumin, and fennel seeds to make marinade.
2. Cut the cod fillet into servings and place it in the marinade.
3. Leave the fish for 30 minutes to marinate.
4. Transfer the fish to the air fryer basket.
5. Cook the fish for 3 minutes at 400F, then flip the fish to another side and cook for 4 minutes more.

Nutrition value/serving: calories 152, fat 4.7, fiber 0.2, carbs 3.4, protein 21.6

Cod Balls

Servings: 2 | **Prep time:** 30 minutes
Cooking time: 6 minutes

Ingredients:

- 7 oz cod fillet, grinded
- 1 tablespoon chives, chopped
- ½ teaspoon minced garlic
- ¼ teaspoon salt
- 1 egg, beaten
- 1 tablespoon almond flour
- Cooking spray

Directions:

1. In the mixing bowl, combine almond flour, beaten egg, salt, garlic, and chives.
2. Mix until homogenous, then add a grinded cod fillet.
3. Form the balls from the fish mixture and put them in the freezer for 10-15 minutes.
4. Transfer the fish balls to the air fryer basket and coat them with cooking spray.
5. Cook the balls for 6 minutes at 400F.

Nutrition value/serving: calories 198, fat 8.8, fiber 0.6, carbs 6.4, protein 23.5

Tilapia Cream

Servings: 4 | **Prep time:** 20 minutes
Cooking time: 9 minutes

Ingredients:

- 11 oz tilapia fillet
- ¼ teaspoon ground nutmeg
- ¼ teaspoon dried oregano
- 1 teaspoon olive oil
- 1 tablespoon avocado oil
- 1 tablespoon dill, chopped
- ½ tablespoon lemon juice
- ½ teaspoon chili powder

Directions:

1. Rub the tilapia fillet with ground nutmeg, oregano, and brush with olive oil.
2. Arrange the fish fillet in the air fryer.
3. Cook the fillet for 7 minutes at 390F.
4. Flip the fillet on another side and cook for 2 minutes more.
5. Transfer the cooked fish fillet to the bowl and shred it.
6. Add avocado oil, dill, lemon juice, and chili powder. Stir the mass well.
7. Refrigerate the pate for 10-15 minutes before serving.

Nutrition value/serving: calories 143, fat 9, fiber 0.3, carbs 0.8, protein 15.4

Garlic Seabass

Servings: 5 | **Prep time:** 15 minutes
Cooking time: 10 minutes

Ingredients:

- 1 ½-pound seabass, trimmed or use 5 big trout fillets
- 1 oz dried thyme
- 4 garlic cloves, peeled, chopped
- 2 tablespoons olive oil
- 1 teaspoon salt

Directions:

1. Rub the seabass with salt and fill it with garlic and thyme.
2. Brush the fish with olive oil and secure the fish cut with a toothpick.
3. Arrange the fish in the air fryer and cook at 375F for 10 minutes.

Nutrition value/serving: calories 316, fat 17.2, fiber 0.1, carbs 2.2, protein 36.5

Fish & Seafood | 43

Curry Shrimps

Servings: 2 | **Prep time:** 10 minutes
Cooking time: 4 minutes

Ingredients:

- 7 oz King shrimp, peeled
- ½ lime
- 1 tablespoon mayonnaise, sugar-free
- ½ teaspoon curry powder
- 1 teaspoon avocado oil

Directions:

1. Sprinkle the shrimp with curry powder and avocado oil, then transfer to the air fryer basket.
2. Cook the shrimp at 400F for 2 minutes on each side.
3. Squeeze the juice of half of the lime over the mayonnaise and whisk well.
4. Transfer the cooked shrimp to the plate and top them with lime-mayonnaise sauce.

Nutrition value/serving: calories 120, fat 4, fiber 1.4, carbs 9, protein 13.3

Nutmeg Scallops

Servings: 2 | **Prep time:** 8 minutes
Cooking time: 4 minutes

Ingredients:

- 9 oz scallops
- ½ teaspoon ground nutmeg
- 1 tablespoon olive oil
- ½ teaspoon ground turmeric
- ½ teaspoon salt
- 1 teaspoon sesame oil

Directions:

1. Season the scallops with ground turmeric, ground nutmeg, and salt, and sprinkle them with sesame oil.
2. Transfer them to the air fryer and cook at 395F for 2 minutes on each side.
3. Place the cooked scallops on the plate and sprinkle them with olive oil.

Nutrition value/serving: calories 186, fat 9.1, fiber 0.3, carbs 3.5, protein 21.6

Cinnamon Shrimps

Servings: 2 | **Prep time:** 20 minutes
Cooking time: 6 minutes

Ingredients:

- 8 oz shrimp, shelled
- 1/3 white onion, sliced
- ¼ teaspoon ground cinnamon
- 1 tablespoon olive oil
- ½ teaspoon salt
- 1 teaspoon chili powder
- 1 teaspoon apple cider vinegar
- 1/3 teaspoon almond flour
- ¼ teaspoon Erythritol

Directions:

1. In the mixing bowl, combine shrimp, onion, ground cinnamon, olive oil, salt, and chili powder. Mix well the shrimp well and leave it for 10 minutes to marinate.
2. Transfer the shrimp mixture to the air fryer and flatten it well.
3. Cook the mixture for 6 minutes at 385F. Stir the ingredients every 2 minutes to avoid burning.
4. In the saucepan, mix Erythritol with apple cider vinegar to make the sauce.
5. Add almond flour and mix the mixture until smooth.
6. Place cooked shrimp on the plate and sprinkle with sauce.

Nutrition value/serving: calories 299, fat 9.1, fiber 1.8, carbs 10.9, protein 27.8

Rosemary Shrimps

Servings: 2 | **Prep time:** 5 minutes
Cooking time: 4 minutes

Ingredients:

- 10 oz shrimp, peeled
- 1 tablespoon sesame oil
- 1 tablespoon lemon juice
- ½ teaspoon dried rosemary

Directions:

1. In the mixing bowl, combine shrimp, sesame oil, and dried rosemary.
2. Transfer them to the air fryer in one layer.
3. Cook the shrimp for 4 minutes at 400F. Shake the shrimp after 3 minutes of cooking.
4. Transfer the cooked seafood to the plate and

sprinkle with lemon juice.

Nutrition value/serving: calories 232, fat 9.4, fiber 0.3, carbs 2.7, protein 32.4

Nutmeg Bites

Servings: 4 | **Prep time:** 30 minutes
Cooking time: 6 minutes

Ingredients:

- 16 tilapia fillets
- 1 tablespoon lemon juice
- ¼ teaspoon salt
- ½ teaspoon ground nutmeg
- 1 tablespoon avocado oil

Directions:

1. Chop the cod fillets roughly and sprinkle them with lemon juice, salt, and ground nutmeg.
2. Mix well and add avocado oil. Stir it and cover it with the foil.
3. Refrigerate the fish mixture for 20 minutes.
4. Preheat the air fryer to 390F.
5. Skew the fish onto the skewers and transfer them to the air fryer basket.
6. Cook the fish for 3 minutes on each side at 390F or until it is golden brown.

Nutrition value/serving: calories 369, fat 4.6, fiber 0.3, carbs 0.9, protein 80.2

Paprika Scallops

Servings: 4 | **Prep time:** 10 minutes
Cooking time: 5 minutes

Ingredients:

- 4 sea scallops
- ¼ teaspoon ground paprika
- 1 teaspoon avocado oil

Directions:

1. Sprinkle the scallops with ground paprika.
2. Skew them on the toothpicks.
3. Sprinkle the scallop skewers with avocado oil and transfer them to the air fryer.
4. Cook the seafood for 5 minutes at 370F.

Nutrition value/serving: calories 80, fat 4.4, fiber 0.1, carbs 1, protein 8.6

Fish Spring Rolls

Servings: 2 | **Prep time:** 10 minutes
Cooking time: 5 minutes

Ingredients:

- 7 oz salmon fillet, cooked
- 1 bell pepper, chopped
- ¼ teaspoon salt
- ½ teaspoon lemon juice
- ½ teaspoon olive oil
- ¼ teaspoon ground black pepper
- 2 wonton wrappers

Directions:

1. In the mixing bowl, combine bell pepper, salt, lemon juice, and ground black pepper.
2. Chop the salmon and add it to the vegetable mixture.
3. Stir the ingredients well.
4. Fill the wonton wrappers with the mixture and roll them up.
5. Brush every roll with olive oil and transfer to the air fryer.
6. Cook the rolls for 5 minutes at 365F.

Nutrition value/serving: calories 262, fat 7.9, fiber 1.6, carbs 25, protein 23.1

Onion Lobsters

Servings: 4 | **Prep time:** 10 minutes
Cooking time: 6

Ingredients:

- 4 lobster tails, trimmed
- 1 teaspoon olive oil
- ½ teaspoon salt
- ¼ teaspoon onion powder
- ½ teaspoon dried dill

Directions:

1. In the mixing bowl, combine dill, onion powder, salt, and olive oil.
2. Rub the lobster tails with the spice mixture well and transfer them to the air fryer.
3. Cook the lobster tails at 395F for 2 minutes on each side.

Nutrition value/serving: calories 183, fat 9.3, fiber 1, carbs 13.3, protein 9.4

Oregano Scallops

Servings: 3 | **Prep time:** 5 minutes
Cooking time: 5 minutes

Ingredients:

- ½ teaspoon dried oregano
- ½ teaspoon lime juice
- ¼ teaspoon lime zest, grated
- 1 tablespoon sesame oil
- 6 scallops

Directions:

1. Rub the scallops with dried oregano, lime juice, and lime zest.
2. Brush the scallops with sesame oil and transfer them to the air fryer.
3. Cook the scallops for 5 minutes at 390F.

Nutrition value/serving: calories 94, fat 5, fiber 0.2, carbs 1.7, protein 10.4

Lime Snapper

Servings: 4 | **Prep time:** 10 minutes
Cooking time: 10 minutes

Ingredients:

- 1-pound snapper, trimmed
- 1 tablespoon dried thyme
- 1 tablespoon olive oil
- 1 teaspoon lime juice
- ½ teaspoon salt

Directions:

1. Rub the snapper with dried thyme and salt.
2. Sprinkle it with lime juice and olive oil.
3. Transfer the fish to the air fryer.
4. Cook it for 5 minutes from each side at 380F.

Nutrition value/serving: calories 182, fat 5.6, fiber 0.3, carbs 0.5, protein 29.8

Lime Dorado

Servings: 5 | **Prep time:** 15 minutes
Cooking time: 18 minutes

Ingredients:

- 1 ½-pounds dorado, trimmed
- 1 tablespoon olive oil
- 1 tablespoon chives, chopped
- 1 lime
- 1 tablespoon fresh dill, chopped
- ½ red onion, diced

Directions:

1. In the mixing bowl, combine olive oil, chives, dill, and onion.
2. Grate the zest from the lime.
3. Squeeze the lime juice into the oil mixture and add grated zest. Stir well.
4. Slice the squeezed lime.
5. Make the diagonal cuts in the Dorado and fill the fish with dill mixture and sliced lime.
6. Transfer the fish to the air fryer and cook at 385F for 18 minutes.

Nutrition value/serving: calories 177, fat 4, fiber 0.7, carbs 2.8, protein.31.5

Olives and Cod

Servings: 4 | **Prep time:** 15 minutes
Cooking time: 15 minutes

Ingredients:

- 16 oz cod fillet
- ½ cup green olives, sliced
- 1 tablespoon olive oil
- ½ teaspoon salt
- 1 teaspoon ground black pepper
- 1 teaspoon ground paprika

Directions:

1. Make the cut (pocket) in the fish fillet.
2. Carefully rub the fish with salt, ground black pepper, paprika, and olive oil.
3. Fill the cod cut with sliced olives and secure it with toothpicks.
4. Transfer the fish fillet to the foil and wrap it.
5. Place the wrapped fillet in the air fryer and cook it at 385F for 15 minutes.

Nutrition value/serving: calories 133, fat 3.8, fiber 0.4, carbs 3.2, protein 20.8

Cayenne Calamari Rings

Servings: 4 | **Prep time:** 10 minutes
Cooking time: 3 minutes

Ingredients:

- 12 oz calamari, washed, trimmed
- ½ teaspoon tomato paste
- 1 teaspoon avocado oil
- ½ teaspoon cayenne pepper
- ¼ teaspoon salt

Directions:
1. Slice the calamari into rings.
2. In the shallow bowl, combine tomato paste, avocado oil, cayenne pepper, and salt.
3. Place the calamari rings in the tomato paste mixture and coat well.
4. Skew the rings onto the wooden skewers and place them in the air fryer.
5. Cook the meal at 400F for 3 minutes.

Nutrition value/serving: calories 184, fat 11.7, fiber 0.1, carbs 13.8, protein 6.1

Coriander Sardines

Servings: 4 | Prep time: 10 minutes
Cooking time: 6 minutes

Ingredients:
- 1-pound sardines, peeled
- ¼ cup fresh dill, chopped
- ¼ cup fresh cilantro, chopped
- ½ teaspoon ground coriander
- ½ teaspoon salt
- ½ teaspoon ground black pepper
- ½ teaspoon chili powder
- 1 tablespoon olive oil
- 1 tablespoon lemon juice

Directions:
1. In the mixing bowl, combine dill, cilantro, coriander, salt, ground black pepper, chili powder, olive oil, and lemon juice.
2. Then place the mixture on ½ part of every sardine. Fold the sardines and transfer them to the air fryer.
3. Close the lid.
4. Cook the fish for 6 minutes at 375F or until the sardines are light brown.

Nutrition value/serving: calories 271, fat 16.7, fiber 0.4, carbs 0.8, protein 28.2

Cumin Grilled Sardines

Servings: 2 | Prep time: 10 minutes
Cooking time: 3 minutes

Ingredients:
- 7 oz sardines, trimmed, peeled
- 1 teaspoon chili powder
- ½ teaspoon salt
- ½ teaspoon ground cumin
- 2 tablespoons water
- 1 teaspoon avocado oil

Directions:
1. In the mixing bowl, combine chili powder, salt, ground cumin, and water.
2. Rub the sardines with the chili powder mixture well and then brush with avocado oil.
3. Transfer the sardines to the air fryer in one layer and cook at 400F for 3 minutes or until they are light brown.

Nutrition value/serving: calories 230, fat 13.9, fiber 0.4, carbs 0.7, protein 24.6

Paprika and Basil Mussels

Servings: 2 | Prep time: 10 minutes
Cooking time: 6 minutes

Ingredients:
- 10 oz blue mussels
- 1 tablespoon ground paprika
- ½ teaspoon dried basil
- 1 teaspoon lemon juice
- ½ teaspoon salt

Directions:
1. In the mixing bowl, combine ground paprika, dried basil, lemon juice, and salt. Whisk the mixture.
2. Sprinkle blue mussels with half of the sauce and mix well.
3. Transfer the mussels to the air fryer and flatten them well.
4. Cook the mussels for 6 minutes at 400F or until they are opened.
5. Transfer the cooked mussels to the bowl and sprinkle with the remaining sauce.

Nutrition value/serving: calories 266, fat 6.9, fiber 0.1, carbs 14.1, protein 33.8

Fenugreek Halibut

Servings: 4 | Prep time: 20 minutes
Cooking time: 20 minutes

Ingredients:
- 1 teaspoon fenugreek seeds
- ¼ onion, minced
- 1 teaspoon olive oil
- 1 teaspoon lemon zest, grated
- ¼ teaspoon ground black pepper
- 2 tablespoons water

- 16 oz halibut fillet
- Cooking spray

Directions:
1. In the shallow bowl, combine minced onion, olive oil, lemon zest, ground black pepper, olive oil, fenugreek seeds, and water.
2. Rub the fish fillet with spice mixture well and leave in the fridge for 15-20 minutes to marinate.
3. Coat the air fryer basket with cooking spray and arrange the halibut fillet inside.
4. Cook the halibut for 20 minutes at 360F. Flip the fillet after 11 minutes of cooking.

Nutrition value/serving: calories 256, fat 6.3, fiber 0.5, carbs 1.7, protein 45.4

Onion Clams

Servings: 3 | **Prep time:** 8 minutes
Cooking time: 14 minutes

Ingredients:
- ¼ teaspoon onion powder
- 1 teaspoon ground nutmeg
- 1 teaspoon olive oil
- ¼ teaspoon dried parsley
- 1 tablespoon lime juice
- 1 tablespoon fish sauce
- ¼ teaspoon kosher salt
- 10 oz clams

Directions:
1. Place the clams in the bowl and sprinkle with onion powder, ground nutmeg, dried parsley, lime juice, and kosher salt.
2. Sprinkle the clams with fish sauce, lime juice, and olive oil. Stir well and transfer to the air fryer.
3. Cook the clams for 14 minutes at 395F. Shake the clams every 6 minutes.

Nutrition value/serving: calories 67, fat 2, fiber 0.6, carbs 11.5, protein 1

Parsley Crayfish

Servings: 4 | **Prep time:** 5 minutes
Cooking time: 7 minutes

Ingredients:
- 14 oz crayfish
- 3 tablespoons olive oil
- ¼ cup fresh parsley, chopped
- 1 teaspoon salt

Directions:
1. Place the crayfish in the air fryer and cook them at 400F for 3 minutes.
2. Whisk together olive oil, parsley, and salt.
3. When the time is over, brush the crayfish generously with the olive oil mixture and cook for 4 more minutes.
4. Transfer the cooked crayfish to the plate and sprinkle them with the remaining oil mixture.

Nutrition value/serving: calories 230, fat 16.8, fiber 0.4, carbs 1.7, protein 18.1

Calamari and Sweet Potato Balls

Servings: 2 | **Prep time:** 15 minutes
Cooking time: 6 minutes

Ingredients:
- 4 oz ground calamari
- 1 teaspoon minced garlic
- ½ teaspoon dried dill
- ½ teaspoon ground coriander
- ¼ cup sweet potato, boiled, mashed
- 1 egg, beaten
- 1/3 cup almond flour
- Cooking spray

Directions:
1. In the bowl, combine ground calamari, minced garlic, dried ill, ground coriander, and mashed sweet potato until homogeneous.
2. Form the balls from it with the help of 2 spoons
3. Dip the balls in the egg and coat them in almond flour.
4. Transfer the meal to the air fryer and spray with cooking spray.
5. Cook the calamari balls for 6 minutes at 385F. Flip them during cooking to avoid burning.

Nutrition value/serving: calories 167, fat 4.9, fiber 1.6, carbs 15.6, protein 9.1

Basil Cod

Servings: 3 | **Prep time:** 10 minutes
Cooking time: 10 minutes

Ingredients:
- 1-pound cod fillet
- 1 lime
- 1 tablespoon dried basil

- 2 tablespoons avocado oil
- ½ teaspoon dried thyme

Directions:
1. Cut the cod fillet into 3 servings.
2. Rub the fish fillets with dried basil and dried thyme.
3. Squeeze the juice of half of the lime over the fillets.
4. Sprinkle the fish with oil and transfer it to the air fryer.
5. Cook the cod at 370F for 5 minutes on each side.
6. If you prefer crunchy crust, increase the cooking time to 13 minutes.
7. Place the cooked cod fillets on the plate and squeeze the juice of the water half of the lime over them.

Nutrition value/serving: calories 146, fat 2.8, fiber 1.5, carbs 21, protein 27.4

Sweet and Sour Cod
Servings: 4 | **Prep time:** 10 minutes
Cooking time: 6 minutes

Ingredients:
- 1 cup kale, chopped
- 1 tablespoon Erythritol
- 1 tablespoon olive oil
- ½ teaspoon chili flakes
- 1 tablespoon lemon juice
- 14 oz cod fillet
- ½ teaspoon salt
- 1 teaspoon ground black pepper
- 1 tablespoon sesame oil

Directions:
1. Sprinkle the cod fillet with salt and ground black pepper.
2. Brush the fish with sesame oil and transfer to the air fryer.
3. Cook the cod for 6 minutes at 400F.
4. Mix kale with olive oil, chili flakes, Erythritol, and lemon. Mix up well.
5. Cool the cooked fish to room temperature and chop roughly.
6. Top the kale mixture with cod.

Nutrition value/serving: calories 163, fat 7.7, fiber 0.5, carbs 4.1, protein 18.4

Zucchini Sardines
Servings: 2 | **Prep time:** 10 minutes
Cooking time: 10 minutes

Ingredients:
- 2 sardines fillets (8 oz sardine fillet)
- 2 teaspoons chives, chopped
- 1 small zucchini, diced
- 1 teaspoon fresh parsley, chopped
- 2 teaspoons sesame oil
- ¼ teaspoon salt

Directions:
1. Blend chives with zucchini, parsley, and 1 teaspoon of sesame oil and salt until smooth.
2. Place the mixture on the sardine fillets and fold them. Secure the fish with toothpicks and brush with the remaining sesame oil.
3. Transfer the sardines to the air fryer.
4. Cook the fish for 10 minutes at 365F. Flip the fish on another side during cooking if desired.

Nutrition value/serving: calories 52, fat 5, fiber 0.2, carbs 0.7, protein 1.2

Garlic Fish Cakes
Servings: 8 | **Prep time:** 20 minutes
Cooking time: 15 minutes

Ingredients:
- 1-pound cod, cooked
- 4 eggs, beaten
- 1 teaspoon salt
- ½ teaspoon cayenne pepper
- ½ cup almond flour
- 1 teaspoon ground black pepper
- 1 teaspoon minced garlic
- 1 tablespoon sesame oil

Directions:
1. Cut the cod into 8 medium pieces.
2. In the mixing bowl, combine eggs, salt, cayenne pepper, ground black pepper, and minced garlic.
3. In a separate bowl put almond flour.
4. Dip the cod pieces in the egg mixture and coat them in almond flour.
5. Arrange the fish in the air fryer in one layer and sprinkle with sesame oil.
6. Cook the cakes for 8 minutes at 365F. Then flip them on another side and cook for 7 minutes more or until they are light brown.

Nutrition value/serving: calories 179, fat 5.9, fiber 0.9, carbs 12.9, protein 17.6

Chili Fish Tacos

Servings: 4 | **Prep time:** 15 minutes
Cooking time: 15 minutes

Ingredients:

- 4 corn tortillas
- ½ cup green cabbage, shredded
- 3 tablespoons lime juice
- ½ teaspoon chili flakes
- 9 oz salmon fillet
- 3 tablespoons Taco seasonings
- 1/3 cup almond flour
- 2 eggs beaten
- 1 teaspoon avocado oil

Directions:

1. In the mixing bowl, combine cabbage, lime juice, and chili flakes. Place the mixture in the fridge for 15 minutes.
2. Cut the salmon fillet into 4 servings and sprinkle each with Taco seasonings.
3. Dip the fish in egg and coat in almond flour.
4. Sprinkle the fish with olive oil and arrange it in the air fryer.
5. Cook the salmon at 365F for 5 minutes on each side.
6. Remove the shredded cabbage mixture from the fridge.
7. Fold the corn tortillas into the envelopes and fill them with cabbage mixture.
8. Add cooked salmon pieces.

Nutrition value/serving: calories 258, fat 11, fiber 2.2, carbs 11.4, protein 18

Coconut Snapper

Servings: 4 | **Prep time:** 10 minutes
Cooking time: 40 minutes

Ingredients:

- 1-pound snapper, trimmed, peeled
- 1 teaspoon dried basil
- 1 tablespoon olive oil
- ½ teaspoon salt
- ½ teaspoon coconut flour

Directions:

1. Rub the snapper with basil and salt.
2. Sprinkle the fish with coconut flour and massage it well.
3. Sprinkle snapper with olive oil and arrange it in the air fryer basket.
4. Close the lid.
5. Cook the meal at 395F for 40 minutes.

Nutrition value/serving: calories 151, fat 2.4, fiber 0.2, carbs 0.8, protein 29.9

POULTRY

Poultry

Lime Chicken

Servings: 4 | Prep time: 10 minutes
Cooking time: 20 minutes

Ingredients:
- 1-pound chicken breast, skinless, boneless
- 1 lime, sliced
- 1 tablespoon coconut milk
- 1 teaspoon ground black pepper
- 1 teaspoon olive oil
- 1 teaspoon salt

Directions:
1. Sprinkle the chicken breast with ground black pepper, olive oil, salt, and coconut milk.
2. Make the cut in the breast and fill it with the sliced lime. Secure the cut with toothpicks.
3. Transfer the chicken breast to the air fryer and cook it at 375F for 10 minutes on both sides.

Nutrition value/serving: calories 139, fat 3.2, fiber 0.6, carbs 1.7, protein 24.3

Paprika Chicken Drumsticks

Servings: 3 | Prep time: 10 minutes
Cooking time: 20 minutes

Ingredients:
- 10 oz chicken drumsticks
- 1 teaspoon salt
- 1 teaspoon ground paprika
- 1 tablespoon olive oil
- 1 teaspoon lemon juice

Directions:
1. Rub the chicken drumsticks with salt, ground paprika, and lemon juice.
2. Brush the chicken drumsticks with olive oil well and transfer them to the air fryer in one layer.
3. Cook the chicken drumsticks for 15 minutes at 385F.
4. Flip the chicken drumsticks on another side and cook for 5 minutes more.

Nutrition value/serving: calories 208, fat 10, fiber 0.3, carbs 2.3, protein 26.1

Chili Pepper Chicken Meatballs

Servings: 4 | Prep time: 10 minutes
Cooking time: 11 minutes

Ingredients:
- 2 cups ground chicken
- 1 teaspoon chili powder
- 2 tablespoons lemon juice
- 1 tablespoon chili flakes
- ½ teaspoon cayenne pepper

Directions:
1. In the mixing bowl, combine ground chicken, chili powder, chili flakes, and cayenne pepper.
2. Make the small meatballs and place them in the air fryer basket.
3. Cook the meatballs for 11 minutes at 400F.
4. Place the cooked meatballs on the plate and sprinkle them with lemon juice.

Nutrition value/serving: calories 336, fat 17, fiber 0.3, carbs 3.1, protein 40.9

Nutmeg Tenders

Servings: 4 | Prep time: 10 minutes
Cooking time: 10 minutes

Ingredients:
- 14 oz chicken fillet
- ¼ cup coconut milk
- 1 teaspoon ground black pepper
- ½ teaspoon ground nutmeg
- ½ cup almond flour
- Cooking spray

Directions:
1. In the mixing bowl, combine coconut milk, ground black pepper, and ground nutmeg. Whisk the mixture until smooth.
2. Cut the chicken fillet into the tenders and dip them in the coconut milk mixture.
3. Coat the chicken tenders in almond flour.
4. Place the tenders in the air fryer and spray them with cooking spray.
5. Cook the chicken tenders at 400F for 5 minutes on each side.

Nutrition value/serving: calories 248, fat 8.2, fiber 0.7, carbs 9.6, protein 31

Tomato Wings

Servings: 2 | **Prep time:** 10 minutes
Cooking time: 18 minutes

Ingredients:

- 8 oz chicken wings
- 1 beefsteak tomato, crushed
- 1 teaspoon sesame oil

Directions:

1. In the shallow bowl, combine sesame oil and crushed tomato.
2. Coat the chicken wings in the tomato mixture.
3. Place the chicken wings in the air fryer and cook them at 375F for 9 minutes on each side.

Nutrition value/serving: calories 244, fat 10.7, fiber 0.7, carbs 1.3, protein 32.8

Italian Seasonings Chicken Thighs

Servings: 2 | **Prep time:** 15 minutes
Cooking time: 14 minutes

Ingredients:

- 8 oz chicken thighs, skinless, boneless
- 1 tablespoon Italian seasonings
- 1 tablespoon avocado oil
- 1 teaspoon lemon juice

Directions:

1. Rub the chicken thighs with Italian seasonings and then sprinkle them with avocado oil and lemon juice.
2. Leave the chicken thighs for 10 minutes to marinate.
3. Transfer the chicken to the air fryer and cook at 390F for 7 minutes on each side.

Nutrition value/serving: calories 276, fat 15.4, fiber 0, carbs 0.1, protein 32.8

Rosemary Whole Chicken

Servings: 10 | **Prep time:** 15 minutes
Cooking time: 60 minutes

Ingredients:

- 4-pounds whole chicken
- 2 tablespoons ground coriander
- 1 tablespoon salt
- 1 tablespoon dried rosemary
- 3 tablespoons olive oil

Directions:

1. Fill the chicken with dried oregano.
2. In the bowl, combine ground coriander, salt, and olive oil.
3. Rub the chicken with the coriander mixture and transfer it to the air fryer.
4. Cook the chicken for 55 minutes at 375F.
5. Flip the chicken on another side and cook for 5 minutes more.

Nutrition value/serving: calories 391, fat 16.7, fiber 0.5, carbs 2.4, protein 52.7

Cumin Chicken Breast

Servings: 4 | **Prep time:** 10 minutes
Cooking time: 33 minutes

Ingredients:

- 10 oz chicken breast, skinless, boneless
- 1 tablespoon ground cumin
- 1 teaspoon dried dill
- ½ teaspoon salt
- 1 teaspoon sunflower oil
- ½ teaspoon ground paprika

Directions:

1. Rub the chicken breast with dried dill, salt, ground cumin, and sunflower oil.
2. Place the chicken breast in the air fryer and cook for 30 minutes at 365F.
3. Flip the chicken and cook it at 360F for 3 more minutes or until crispy.

Nutrition value/serving: calories 133, fat 3.8, fiber 0.7, carbs 5.1, protein 15.8

Parsley Liver Pate

Servings: 4 | **Prep time:** 10 minutes
Cooking time: 8 minutes

Ingredients:

- 3 tablespoons coconut milk
- 1 teaspoon salt
- 1 carrot, boiled
- 1 tablespoon fresh parsley, chopped
- 1 teaspoon olive oil
- 12 oz chicken liver

Directions:

1. Sprinkle the chicken liver with olive oil and place in the air fryer.
2. Cook it for 8 minutes at 395F.

Poultry Recipes | 53

3. Transfer the cooked liver to the blender.
4. Add salt, coconut milk, carrot, and parsley.
5. Blend the mixture until smooth.
6. Transfer the cooked pate to the bowl and store it in the fridge for up to 7 days.

Nutrition value/serving: calories 238, fat 15.4, fiber 0.5, carbs 1.7, protein 21.2

Sage Turkey

Servings: 4 | **Prep time:** 10 minutes
Cooking time: 40 minutes

Ingredients:

- 15 oz turkey breast, boneless
- 1 teaspoon sage
- 1 teaspoon salt
- 1 teaspoon ground black pepper
- 1 tablespoon olive oil

Directions:

1. Rub the breast with sage, salt, ground black pepper, and olive oil.
2. Place the turkey breast in the air fryer and cook it at 380F for 40 minutes.
3. Slice the cooked turkey breast into pieces.

Nutrition value/serving: calories 116, fat 2.2, fiber 0.9, carbs 4.1, protein 18.3

Chives Patties

Servings: 4 | **Prep time:** 15 minutes
Cooking time: 12 minutes

Ingredients:

- 1 cup ground chicken
- 4 tablespoons almond flour
- 1 teaspoon chives, chopped
- 1 teaspoon chili powder
- 1 teaspoon avocado oil

Directions:

1. In the mixing bowl, combine ground chicken, almond flour, chives, and chili powder.
2. Form the medium size cakes from the ground chicken mixture.
3. Transfer the chicken cakes to the air fryer and sprinkle them lightly with avocado oil.
4. Cook the cakes for 8 minutes at 375F.
5. Flip the patties on another side and cook them for 4 minutes more or until they are golden brown.

Nutrition value/serving: calories 119, fat 4.6, fiber 0.5, carbs 5.5, protein 13.4

Chicken Breast Boats

Servings: 4 | **Prep time:** 15 minutes
Cooking time: 25 minutes

Ingredients:

- 1-pound chicken breast, skinless, boneless
- 1 teaspoon dried dill
- 1 teaspoon salt
- ½ teaspoon minced garlic
- ½ teaspoon paprika
- ½ teaspoon sage
- 1 teaspoon olive, melted

Directions:

1. In the mixing bowl, combine, dried dill, salt, minced garlic, paprika, and sage.
2. Cut the chicken breast into the shape of a Hasselback and brush them with the garlic mixture.
3. Wrap the chicken in the foil.
4. Place the chicken breast in the air fryer and cook it for 25 minutes at 375F.

Nutrition value/serving: calories 168, fat 5.6, fiber 0.3, carbs 0.9, protein 24.4

Onion Chicken

Servings: 8 | **Prep time:** 15 minutes
Cooking time: 12 minutes

Ingredients:

- 2-pound chicken fillet
- ½ cup coconut milk
- 1 teaspoon salt
- 1 tablespoon onion powder
- ½ teaspoon chili powder
- ½ cup almond flour
- 1 tablespoon sunflower oil

Directions:

1. Chop the chicken fillet into small cubes.
2. In the mixing bowl, combine coconut milk, salt, onion powder, and chili powder.
3. Dip the chicken popcorn in the coconut milk mixture and coat them with almond flour, then transfer it to the air fryer basket.
4. Sprinkle the popcorn with sunflower oil.
5. Cook the popcorn chicken at 375F for 12 minutes. Shake the popcorn every 3 minutes.

Nutrition value/serving: calories 267, fat 10.5, fiber 0.4, carbs 5.1, protein 34.2

Garlic Chicken

Servings: 4 | **Prep time:** 10 minutes
Cooking time: 12 minutes

Ingredients:

- 8 oz chicken wings, skinless, boneless
- ½ teaspoon salt
- 1 egg, beaten
- 1 teaspoon ground garlic
- Cooking spray

Directions:

1. Dip the chicken wings in an egg.
2. Sprinkle the chicken with ground garlic and salt.
3. Coat the chicken wings with cooking spray and cook them for 12 minutes at 200F or until they are light brown.

Nutrition value/serving: calories 171, fat 6.1, fiber 1, carbs 8, protein 19.8

Oregano Chicken Fillets

Servings: 4 | **Prep time:** 10 minutes
Cooking time: 15 minutes

Ingredients:

- 1-pound chicken fillet
- 1 teaspoon dried oregano
- 1 tablespoon olive oil
- 1 tablespoon water

Directions:

1. Cut the chicken fillet into 4 servings and mix up with oregano, olive oil, and water.
2. Place the chicken fillets in the air fryer in one layer and cook them for 15 minutes at 365F. Flip the fillets on another side after 10 minutes of cooking.

Nutrition value/serving: calories 247, fat 12, fiber 0.2, carbs 0.3, protein 32.9

Marjoram Chicken Shred

Servings: 3 | **Prep time:** 15 minutes
Cooking time: 14 minutes

Ingredients:

- 9 oz chicken fillet
- 1 teaspoon dried marjoram
- 1 teaspoon avocado oil
- ½ teaspoon chili flakes
- 1 teaspoon ground black pepper
- 1 teaspoon sunflower oil

Directions:

1. Cut the chicken fillet into 3 servings.
2. Place the chicken fillets in the air fryer and sprinkle them with sunflower oil.
3. Cook the chicken for 14 minutes at 375F. Flip the chicken in halfway through cooking.
4. In the mixing bowl, combine dried marjoram, avocado oil, chili flakes, and ground black pepper.
5. Shred the cooked chicken with the forks and add the spice mixture. Mix well

Nutrition value/serving: calories 194, fat 9.5, fiber 0.3, carbs 1.1, protein 24.8

Spicy Chicken

Servings: 5 | **Prep time:** 15 minutes
Cooking time: 12 minutes

Ingredients:

- 15 oz chicken breast, skinless, boneless, chopped
- 1 tablespoon almond flour
- ½ teaspoon salt
- 1 tablespoon sriracha sauce
- 1 tablespoon olive oil
- 1 teaspoon avocado oil

Directions:

1. In the mixing bowl, combine chopped chicken and almond flour. Sprinkle the chicken with avocado oil.
2. Transfer the chicken to the air fryer and cook it for 12 minutes at 400F. Shake the chicken every 3 minutes during cooking. The cooking time depends on the chicken pieces' size.
3. In the saucepan, mix salt with sriracha sauce and olive oil.
4. Sprinkle the cooked chicken with sauce and stir well.

Nutrition value/serving: calories 156, fat 7.1, fiber 0.1, carbs 3.1, protein 18.5

Coated Chicken

Servings: 4 | **Prep time:** 10 minutes
Cooking time: 20 minutes

Ingredients:

- 10 oz chicken fillet
- 4 teaspoons almond flour
- 1 teaspoon ground black pepper
- ½ teaspoon chili powder

Poultry Recipes | 55

- ½ teaspoon salt
- 2 eggs, beaten
- 1 teaspoon olive oil

Directions:

1. Whisk eggs with salt, chili powder, and ground black pepper.
2. Cut the chicken into 4 servings and place it in the egg mixture.
3. Coat each chicken piece in almond flour and place it in the air fryer in one layer.
4. Sprinkle the chicken with olive oil and cook it at 365F for 20 minutes. Flip the chicken from time to time to avoid burning.

Nutrition value/serving: calories 188, fat 8.9, fiber 0.3, carbs 2.2, protein 23.7

Yellow Fillets

Servings: 2 | **Prep time:** 15 minutes
Cooking time: 12 minutes

Ingredients:

- ½ teaspoon turmeric
- 1 tablespoon olive oil
- 8 oz chicken fillet

Directions:

1. Cut the chicken fillet into 2 steaks.
2. Rub the chicken with turmeric and sprinkle with olive oil.
3. Arrange the chicken fillets in the air fryer and cook them for 6 minutes on each side at 385F.

Nutrition value/serving: calories 228, fat 9.4, fiber 0.6, carbs 1.1, protein 33

Egg Chicken Fillets

Servings: 4 | **Prep time:** 15 minutes
Cooking time: 6 minutes

Ingredients:

- 1-pound chicken fillet
- 2 eggs, beaten
- 1 teaspoon salt
- 1 tablespoon avocado oil

Directions:

1. Slice the chicken fillet into 4 servings.
2. Dip every chicken piece in the egg mixture, then sprinkle with salt.
3. Place the chicken in the air fryer and drizzle with avocado oil.
4. Cook the meal at 375F for 3 minutes on each side.

Nutrition value/serving: calories 305, fat 14.5, fiber 0.4, carbs 5.4, protein 36.5

Chicken and Kalamata Olives

Servings: 2 | **Prep time:** 10 minutes
Cooking time: 13 minutes

Ingredients:

- ½ cup Kalamata olives
- 1 cup cucumber, chopped
- 1 cup lettuce, chopped
- 2 tablespoons olive oil
- 2 tablespoons lemon juice
- 1 teaspoon ground cumin
- ½ teaspoon ground cinnamon
- 1 teaspoon ground coriander
- 1 teaspoon dried cilantro
- 1 tablespoon Greek yogurt
- 2 chicken thighs, skinless, boneless

Directions:

1. Chop the chicken thighs roughly and sprinkle them with dried cilantro, coriander, cinnamon, olive oil, and cumin.
2. Mix well and transfer the chicken to the air fryer.
3. Cook the chicken for 13 minutes at 375F. Stir the chicken every 2 minutes.
4. In the mixing bowl, combine Kalamata olives, cucumber, and lettuce.
5. Sprinkle the vegetables with lemon juice and stir well.
6. Transfer the mixture to the serving bowls.
7. Top the vegetable mixture with cooked chicken and sprinkle with Greek yogurt.

Nutrition value/serving: calories 541, fat 36.2, fiber 3.2, carbs 9.6, protein 45.1

Tender Chicken Strips

Servings: 4 | **Prep time:** 20 minutes
Cooking time: 10 minutes

- 11 oz chicken fillet
- 1 tablespoon white pepper
- 1 teaspoon avocado oil

Directions:

1. Cut the chicken fillet into strips.
2. In the shallow bowl, combine avocado oil and white pepper.

3. When the mixture is smooth, pour it over the chicken strips and mix well.
4. Leave the chicken for 15 minutes to marinate.
5. Transfer the chicken strips to the air fryer and flatten them in one layer.
6. Cook chicken strips at 385F for 5 minutes on each side.

Nutrition value/serving: calories 190, fat 9.8, fiber 0, carbs 1.2, protein 22.8

Greens Wraps

Servings: 4 | **Prep time:** 10 minutes
Cooking time: 17 minutes

Ingredients:

- 14 oz chicken drumsticks
- 5 oz spinach leaves
- 1 teaspoon dried oregano
- 1 tablespoon olive oil

Directions:

1. Rub the chicken drumsticks with dried oregano.
2. Wrap each chicken drumstick in the spinach leaves and transfer to the air fryer.
3. Cook the chicken drumsticks at 365F for 15 minutes (flip the drumsticks on another side after 10 minutes of cooking.
4. Sprinkle the greens wraps with olive oil and cook for 2 additional minutes.

Nutrition value/serving: calories 259, fat 11.4, fiber 0.1, carbs 2.3, protein 34.8

Mustard Chicken Tenders

Servings: 7 | **Prep time:** 15 minutes
Cooking time: 17 minutes

Ingredients:

- 3-pounds chicken breast, skinless, boneless
- 3 tablespoons mustard
- 1 tablespoon olive oil

Directions:

1. Chop the chicken breast into the cubes and combine them with mustard and olive oil.
2. Let it sit for 10 minutes in the fridge.
3. Transfer the chicken to the air fryer and flatten gently with the spatula.
4. Cook the meal for 17 minutes at 360F.

Nutrition value/serving: calories 257, fat 6.9, fiber 0, carbs 3.2, protein 42.4

Cucumber and Chicken Sandwich

Servings: 2 | **Prep time:** 15 minutes
Cooking time: 10 minutes

Ingredients:

- 8 spinach leaves
- 6 oz chicken fillet
- 1 tablespoon mayonnaise, sugar-free
- 1 teaspoon ground black pepper
- 1 English cucumber, sliced
- 1 teaspoon sunflower oil

Directions:

1. In the mixing bowl, combine the sunflower oil and ground black pepper.
2. Cut the chicken fillet into 2 servings and rub it with the oil mixture.
3. Place the chicken fillets in the air fryer and cook them for 5 minutes on each side at 390F.
4. Place the cooked chicken fillet on the 2 spinach leaves.
5. Top the chicken with sliced cucumber and mayonnaise.
6. Cover the sandwich with 2 more spinach leaves.
7. Repeat the same steps with the remaining ingredients.

Nutrition value/serving: calories 337, fat 20.7, fiber 0.7, carbs 4.6, protein 32.2

Yogurt Chicken Wings

Servings: 2 | **Prep time:** 10 minutes
Cooking time: 10 minutes

Ingredients:

- 4 chicken wings, skinless, boneless
- 1 tablespoon lime juice
- ½ cup Greek yogurt
- 1 teaspoon ground coriander
- 1 teaspoon avocado oil

Directions:

1. Whisk lime juice with Greek yogurt, ground coriander, and avocado oil.
2. Carefully brush every chicken wing with the lime mixture and transfer them to the air fryer.
3. Cook the chicken wings for 7 minutes at 365F.
4. Flip the chicken wings to another side and cook for 3 additional minutes at 400F.

Nutrition value/serving: calories 51, fat 1.5, fiber 0.2, carbs 0.6, protein 8.4

Jalapeno Chicken Tights

Servings: 4 | **Prep time:** 10 minutes
Cooking time: 20 minutes

Ingredients:

- 4 chicken thighs, skinless, boneless
- 1/3 cup fresh dill, chopped
- ½ lemon
- 2 jalapeno peppers
- 1 tablespoon olive oil
- ½ teaspoon salt

Directions:

1. Put the chicken thighs in the bowl.
2. Squeeze the juice of half of the lemon over the chicken thighs.
3. Grind dill and jalapeno pepper, and add the mixture to the chicken.
4. Add salt and olive oil.
5. Mix the poultry well and leave it for 20 minutes to marinate.
6. Place the marinated chicken thighs in the air fryer and cook them at 365°F for 10 minutes on each side.

Nutrition value/serving: calories 311, fat 14.3, fiber 0.4, carbs 1.2, protein 42.5

Celery Chicken Thighs

Servings: 2 | **Prep time:** 10 minutes
Cooking time: 20 minutes

Ingredients:

- 2 chicken thighs
- 2 oz celery root, grated
- 1 tablespoon lime juice
- 1 tablespoon avocado oil
- ½ teaspoon salt

Directions:

1. Mix grated celery root with lime juice, salt, and avocado oil.
2. Carefully rub the chicken thighs with the celery root mixture. Leave the poultry for 20 minutes to marinate.
3. Transfer the chicken thighs to the air fryer and cook for 20 minutes at 365F.

Nutrition value/serving: calories 306, fat 12.1, fiber 1.5, carbs 4.1, protein 43

Almond Chicken Tenders

Servings: 4 | **Prep time:** 10 minutes
Cooking time: 12 minutes

Ingredients:

- 11 oz chicken fillet
- 5 almonds, chopped
- ¼ cup almond flour
- 1 egg, beaten
- ½ teaspoon salt
- 1 teaspoon olive oil

Directions:

1. Cut the chicken into tenders and sprinkle them with salt.
2. Dip the chicken tenders in egg well.
3. Combine chopped almonds with almond flour.
4. Coat each chicken tender in the almond mixture.
5. Transfer the chicken tenders to the air fryer and sprinkle them with olive oil.
6. Cook the meal at 390F for 6 minutes on each side.

Nutrition value/serving: calories 368, fat 23.9, fiber 2.2, carbs 8, protein 31.3

Tender Chicken Breast

Servings: 6 | **Prep time:** 10 minutes
Cooking time: 40 minutes

Ingredients:

- 18 oz chicken breast, boneless
- 1 teaspoon ground paprika
- 1 tablespoon olive oil

Directions:

1. Make the small cuts in chicken breast and sprinkle them with olive oil.
2. Rub the chicken with ground paprika and transfer it to the air fryer.
3. Cook the meal for 30 minutes at 385F.
4. Then flip the chicken on another side and cook for 10 minutes more.

Nutrition value/serving: calories 119, fat 4.5, fiber 0.3, carbs 0.4, protein 18.1

Oregano Chicken Sausage

Servings: 3 | **Prep time:** 5 minutes
Cooking time: 8 minutes

Ingredients:

- 3 chicken sausages
- 1 teaspoon olive oil
- ½ teaspoon dried oregano

Directions:

1. Sprinkle the chicken sausages with olive oil and dried oregano and arrange them in the air fryer basket.
2. Cook the chicken sausages at 375F for 4 minutes on each side.

Nutrition value/serving: calories 90, fat 6, fiber 0.4, carbs 2.9, protein 5.3

Thyme and Garlic Whole Chicken

Servings: 10 | **Prep time:** 20 minutes
Cooking time: 60 minutes

Ingredients:

- 3-pounds whole chicken
- 1 teaspoon minced garlic
- 1 teaspoon dried thyme
- 2 tablespoons sesame oil

Directions:

1. Rub the chicken with minced garlic and dried thyme.
2. Sprinkle the chicken with sesame oil.
3. Place the chicken in the air fryer.
4. Cook the meal for 60 minutes at 385F.

Nutrition value/serving: calories 514, fat 34.6, fiber 0.6, carbs 1.7, protein 37.8

Tomato Chicken Wings

Servings: 4 | **Prep time:** 10 minutes
Cooking time: 9 minutes

Ingredients:

- ½ teaspoon minced garlic
- ½ cup cherry tomatoes, crushed
- 1 teaspoon lemon juice
- ½ teaspoon sesame oil
- ¼ teaspoon ground cumin
- ½ teaspoon dried oregano
- 1-pound chicken wings

Directions:

1. Place the chicken wings in the bowl.
2. Sprinkle them with crushed tomatoes, lemon juice, sesame oil, ground cumin, and dried oregano. Mix well.
3. Arrange the chicken wings in the air fryer in one layer.
4. Cook the wings for 9 minutes at 400F.

Nutrition value/serving: calories 231, fat 9.1, fiber 0.4, carbs 1.7, protein 33.7

Chicken and Onion Bowl

Servings: 2 | **Prep time:** 10 minutes
Cooking time: 17 minutes

Ingredients:

- 9 oz chicken fillet, chopped
- 1 white onion, sliced
- 1 tablespoon Italian seasonings
- 1 teaspoon sesame oil

Directions:

1. Sprinkle the chopped chicken fillet with Italian seasonings and transfer it to the air fryer basket.
2. Add sliced onion and sesame oil and stir well.
3. Cook the chicken for 17 minutes at 355F.
4. Shake the meal every 5 minutes during cooking.

Nutrition value/serving: calories 322, fat 12.1, fiber 2.8, carbs 14.1, protein 38.7

Chicken and Asparagus

Servings: 5 | **Prep time:** 10 minutes
Cooking time: 5 minutes

Ingredients:

- 5 corn tortillas
- 1-pound chicken breast, cooked
- 3 oz asparagus, boiled, chopped
- 1 teaspoon olive oil
- 1 oz cottage cheese

Directions:

1. Shred the cooked chicken breast with the fork and mix it with cottage cheese and asparagus.
2. Place the shredded chicken mixture on each tortilla and roll them up.
3. Brush the rolled tortillas with olive oil and transfer them to the air fryer.
4. Cook the meal for 5 minutes at 400F or until they

are golden brown.

Nutrition value/serving: calories 202, fat 5.4, fiber 2.4, carbs 16.6, protein 21.9

Greek Style Chicken Breast

Servings: 4 | **Prep time:** 15 minutes
Cooking time: 15 minutes

Ingredients:

- 18 oz chicken breast, skinless, boneless, chopped
- ½ cup Greek yogurt
- ½ teaspoon salt
- 4 garlic cloves, diced
- 1 tablespoon avocado oil

Directions:

1. Place the chopped chicken breast in the bowl.
2. Add Greek yogurt, salt, garlic cloves, and avocado oil. Mix everything well.
3. Leave the chicken to marinate for at least 15 minutes.
4. Transfer the chicken cubes to the air fryer and cook them for 15 minutes at 375F.
5. Stir the chicken cubes every 5 minutes to avoid burning.

Nutrition value/serving: calories 197, fat 6.6, fiber 0.3, carbs 3.4, protein 29.2

Fenugreek and Dill Chicken

Servings: 2 | **Prep time:** 10 minutes
Cooking time: 12 minutes

Ingredients:

- ½ cup ground chicken
- 1 tablespoon dried fenugreek
- 4 tablespoons fresh dill, chopped
- 1 teaspoon sunflower oil

Directions:

1. In the mixing bowl, combine ground chicken, dill, and fenugreek.
2. Form the small fingers from the chicken mixture with your fingertips.
3. Place the fingers in the air fryer, sprinkle with sunflower oil, and cook them at 375°F for 6 minutes on each side.
4. The cooked chicken fingers should be golden brown.

Nutrition value/serving: calories 276, fat 20.7, fiber 1, carbs 5.2, protein 22.1

Oats Chicken Balls

Servings: 4 | **Prep time:** 10 minutes
Cooking time: 8 minutes

Ingredients:

- 9 oz chicken fillet
- 1 jalapeno
- 1 tablespoon water
- 4 tablespoons cut oats
- 1 teaspoon olive oil
- ½ teaspoon salt

Directions:

1. Grind the chicken fillet and jalapeno pepper until smooth.
2. Add water, cut oats, and salt, and stir the mixture until homogeneous.
3. Form the balls from the chicken mixture and transfer them to the air fryer.
4. Sprinkle the balls with olive oil.
5. Cook the balls for 8 minutes at 400F.

Nutrition value/serving: calories 162, fat 6.2, fiber 0.6, carbs 2.7, protein 19.2

Hot Chili Flakes Chicken

Servings: 4 | **Prep time:** 10 minutes
Cooking time: 15 minutes

Ingredients:

- 8 oz chicken fillet, chopped
- 1 teaspoon chili flakes
- ¼ cup water
- 1 tablespoon olive oil
- 1 onion, sliced
- Cooking spray

Directions:

1. Place the chicken in the bowl and sprinkle with chili flakes and olive oil.
2. Stir the chicken well. Transfer the chicken to the air fryer basket and coat it with cooking spray.
3. Add water and stir the mass until smooth.
4. Cook the chicken for 15 minutes at 375F. Stir the chicken every 5 minutes.

Nutrition value/serving: calories 147, fat 4.7, fiber 1.4, carbs 7.7, protein 17.6

Dill Chicken Cutlets

Servings: 4 | **Prep time:** 10 minutes
Cooking time: 18 minutes

Ingredients:

- 4 chicken cutlets
- 1 teaspoon olive oil
- 1 teaspoon dried dill

Directions:

1. Brush the chicken cutlets with olive oil and sprinkle with dried dill.
2. Preheat the air fryer to 355F and place the chicken cutlets inside.
3. Cook them at 355F for 9 minutes on each side.

Nutrition value/serving: calories 501, fat 25.4, fiber 0.5, carbs 4.7, protein 59.2

Chicken and Tofu Pizza

Servings: 4 | **Prep time:** 20 minutes
Cooking time: 16 minutes

Ingredients:

- 2 chicken thighs, skinless, boneless
- 1 cherry tomato, crushed
- ¼ cup tofu, crumbled
- 1 teaspoon curry powder

Directions:

1. Cut every chicken thigh into halves.
2. Make diagonal cuts in every chicken thigh half.
3. Spread the chicken cuts with crushed tomato.
4. Sprinkle them with curry powder.
5. Fill the chicken thigh cuts with tofu.
6. Secure the cuts with toothpicks and transfer them to the air fryer.
7. Cook the pizzas at 385°F for 8 minutes from each side.

Nutrition value/serving: calories 267, fat 15.7, fiber 0.3, carbs 1.8, protein 28.6

Coriander Duck Breast

Servings: 4 | **Prep time:** 10 minutes
Cooking time: 14 minutes

Ingredients:

- 11 oz duck breast, skinless, boneless
- 1/3 cup cranberry juice, freshly squeezed
- 1 teaspoon ground coriander
- ½ teaspoon ground black pepper
- 1 teaspoon olive oil

Directions:

1. Rub the duck breast with ground black pepper and olive oil.
2. Transfer the duck to the air fryer.
3. Cook the duck breast for 14 minutes at 400F.
4. Flip the duck breast on another side and cook it for 7 minutes more.
5. Pour cranberry juice into the saucepan and bring to a boil.
6. Add ground coriander and whisk the liquid well.
7. Remove the sauce from the heat.
8. Slice the cooked duck breast and transfer it to the plate.
9. Sprinkle the duck breast with cranberry sauce.

Nutrition value/serving: calories 121, fat 4.3, fiber 0.6, carbs 1.9, protein 17.2

Oregano Duck Drumsticks

Servings: 4 | **Prep time:** 10 minutes
Cooking time: 18 minutes

Ingredients:

- 4 duck drumsticks
- 1 tablespoon olive oil
- 1 tablespoon dried oregano

Directions:

1. Mix olive oil with oregano.
2. Brush each drumstick with oregano mixture and transfer to the air fryer.
3. Cook the duck drumsticks at 360°F for 9 minutes on each side.

Nutrition value/serving: calories 243, fat 15.3, fiber 0.5, carbs 0.8, protein 23.1

Fragrant Whole Chicken

Servings: 6 | **Prep time:** 15 minutes
Cooking time: 40 minutes

Ingredients:

- 1 ½-pounds whole chicken
- 2 teaspoons olive oil
- ½ teaspoon ground ginger
- ½ teaspoon garlic powder
- ¼ teaspoon Erythritol
- 1 tablespoon almond flour
- 1 teaspoon ground coriander

Directions:

1. In the mixing bowl, combine ground ginger, garlic powder, Erythritol, almond flour, and ground coriander.
2. Rub the chicken with olive oil.
3. Sprinkle it with a ginger mixture.
4. Place the chicken in the air fryer and cook it for 40 minutes at 360F.

Nutrition value/serving: calories 237, fat 9.8, fiber 0, carbs 1.7, protein 32.9

Coconut Duck Cream

Servings: 4 | **Prep time:** 10 minutes
Cooking time: 14 minutes

Ingredients:

- ¼ cup coconut cream
- ¼ cup fresh parsley, chopped
- 12 oz duck breast, skinless, boneless
- 1 teaspoon olive oil
- 1 teaspoon salt
- 1 teaspoon white pepper

Directions:

1. Brush the duck breast with olive oil and sprinkle with white pepper.
2. Place it in the air fryer and cook at 375F for 14 minutes.
3. Shred the cooked duck breast and transfer it to the blender.
4. Blend until smooth.
5. Transfer the smooth duck mixture to the bowl.
6. Add salt, parsley, and coconut cream, then stir gently.

Nutrition value/serving: calories 147, fat 6.8, fiber 0.6, carbs 2.1, protein 19.5

Garlic Duck Meatballs

Servings: 5 | **Prep time:** 20 minutes
Cooking time: 14 minutes

Ingredients:

- 6 oz duck, grinded
- 3 oz ground beef
- 1 teaspoon minced garlic
- 1 tablespoon Italian seasonings
- 1 teaspoon olive oil
- 2 tablespoons almond flour

Directions:

1. In the mixing bowl, combine ground duck and ground beef.
2. Add minced garlic, Italian seasonings, and almond flour, then mix well.
3. Form the meatballs from the meat mixture.
4. Place them in the freezer for 15 minutes.
5. Transfer the meatballs to the air fryer in one layer.
6. Sprinkle the meatballs with olive oil.
7. Cook the meatballs for 14 minutes at 360F.

Nutrition value/serving: calories 208, fat 12.5, fiber 0.7, carbs 4.2, protein 18

Cayenne Pepper Duck Wings

Servings: 4 | **Prep time:** 8 minutes
Cooking time: 20 minutes

Ingredients:

- 4 duck wings
- ¼ cup coconut milk
- 1 teaspoon cayenne pepper
- 1 teaspoon olive oil
- 1 teaspoon salt

Directions:

1. Place the duck wings in the baking pan.
2. Sprinkle the wings with cayenne pepper, salt, olive oil, and coconut milk.
3. Shake the mixture gently. Cover the baking pan with foil.
4. Transfer the baking pan to the air fryer.
5. Cook the duck wings for 20 minutes at 355F.

Nutrition value/serving: calories 123, fat 8.3, fiber 0.1, carbs 1.2, protein 9.8

Mustard and Mayo Chicken

Servings: 6 | **Prep time:** 20 minutes
Cooking time: 18 minutes

Ingredients:

- 3 chicken fillets
- 1 teaspoon mayonnaise, sugar-free
- 1 teaspoon mustard
- 3 eggs, beaten

Directions:

1. Cut every chicken fillet into halves horizontally.
2. Beat every fillet with the kitchen hammer.

3. Rub the chicken fillets with mayonnaise and mustard.
4. Dip the chicken fillets in the egg.
5. Transfer the chicken to the air fryer.
6. Cook the meal at 365F for 18 minutes. Flip the chicken every 3 minutes to avoid burning.

Nutrition value/serving: calories 308, fat 13.4, fiber 0.8, carbs 12.2, protein 31.9

Spinach and Turkey Mix

Servings: 4 | **Preparation time:** 10 minutes
Cooking time: 20 minutes

Ingredients:
- 2 pounds ground turkey breast, skinless, boneless
- 1 cup fresh spinach, chopped
- 1 yellow onion, sliced
- 1 teaspoon basil, dried
- 1 cup tomato sauce
- 1 tablespoon parsley, chopped

Directions:
1. In the air fryer's pan, combine all the ingredients, insert the pan to the air fryer, and cook at 370°F for 20 minutes.
2. Transfer the meal into bowls and serve hot.

Nutrition value/serving: Calories 283, fat 8, fiber 5, carbs 14, protein 20

Chili Poppers

Servings: 4 | **Prep time:** 15 minutes
Cooking time: 10 minutes

Ingredients:
- 4 chili pepper
- 5 oz ground duck
- 1 teaspoon mayonnaise, sugar-free
- 1 teaspoon olive oil

Directions:
1. In the mixing bowl, combine ground duck and mayonnaise.
2. Cut the chili peppers lengthwise into halves and remove the seeds.
3. Fill the chili peppers with duck mixture and sprinkle with olive oil. Wrap them in the foil.
4. Cook the chili poppers for 10 minutes at 375F.

Nutrition value/serving: calories 164, fat 9.8, fiber 0.2, carbs 1.5, protein 15.8

VEGETABLE MEALS

Vegetable Meals

Cilantro Corn on Cobs

Servings: 4 | **Prep time:** 7 minutes
Cooking time: 10 minutes

Ingredients:
- 4 corn on the cobs
- 1 teaspoon dried cilantro
- 1 tablespoon olive oil
- Cooking spray

Directions:
1. Rub the corn on cobs with dried cilantro and place in the air fryer. Coat the corn with cooking spray.
2. Cook the corn at 400°F for 5 minutes on each side.
3. When the corn on the cobs is cooked, brush it gently with olive oil.

Nutrition value/serving: calories 88, fat 3.5, fiber 2, carbs 14.8, protein 2.1

Lime Broccoli

Servings: 2 | **Prep time:** 10 minutes
Cooking time: 10 minutes

Ingredients:
- 1 pecan, chopped
- 1 cup broccoli florets, roughly chopped
- 1 teaspoon olive oil
- 1 teaspoon soy sauce
- ½ teaspoon Erythritol
- 1 teaspoon lime juice
- ½ teaspoon minced garlic

Directions:
1. Place the broccoli in the air fryer and sprinkle it with olive oil.
2. Cook the broccoli for 10 minutes at 400F. Stir the vegetables every 2 minutes to avoid burning.
3. Whisk together chopped pecan, soy sauce, Erythritol, lime juice, and minced garlic to make the sauce.
4. Place the cooked meal on the serving plates and sprinkle it with sauce. Stir gently.

Nutrition value/serving: calories 128, fat 9.4, fiber 2.4, carbs 6.4, protein 5.2

Carrot Mix

Servings: 5 | **Prep time:** 5 minutes
Cooking time: 30 minutes

Ingredients:
- 2 cups broccoli, chopped
- ½ cup Brussels sprouts
- ½ cup carrot, chopped
- ½ cup butternut squash, peeled, chopped
- 1 teaspoon salt
- 1 teaspoon dried oregano
- 1 tablespoon sunflower oil

Directions:
1. Put broccoli and Brussels sprouts in the air fryer.
2. Cook the vegetables for 10 minutes at 370°F. Stir the vegetables halfway through cooking.
3. Transfer the cooked vegetables to the mixing bowl.
4. Place the carrot and butternut squash in the air fryer and cook them for 20 minutes at 375°F. Stir the vegetables every 5 minutes.
5. Add the cooked carrot and butternut squash to other cooked vegetables.
6. Sprinkle them with sunflower oil, dried oregano, and salt, then stir everything well.

Nutrition value/serving: calories 69, fat 3, fiber 2.1, carbs 5.4, protein 1.4

Chili Squash

Servings: 4 | **Prep time:** 15 minutes
Cooking time: 10 minutes

Ingredients:
- 14 oz butternut squash
- 1 tablespoon olive oil
- 1 teaspoon chili powder

Directions:
1. Cut the butternut squash into the sig zag sticks and place it in the air fryer.
2. Add olive oil and chili powder.
3. Stir the butternut squash well and cook for 10 minutes at 385F. Shake the vegetables every 2 minutes to avoid burning.

Nutrition value/serving: calories 78, fat 3.6, fiber 2.2, carbs 5.3, protein 1.1

Garlic Cauliflower Head

Servings: 4 | **Prep time:** 10 minutes
Cooking time: 15 minutes

Ingredients:

- 1-pound cauliflower head, trimmed
- 2 tablespoons Greek yogurt
- ½ teaspoon ground black pepper
- ½ teaspoon garlic powder

Directions:

1. In the mixing bowl, combine Greek yogurt, ground black pepper, and garlic powder.
2. Brush the cauliflower head with the Greek yogurt mixture and place it in the air fryer.
3. Cook the vegetable for 15 minutes at 360F.
4. Cool the cooked cauliflower head a little, then cut it into servings.

Nutrition value/serving: calories 72, fat 3.3, fiber 2.9, carbs 5.9, protein 4.3

Coriander Asparagus

Servings: 3 | **Prep time:** 5 minutes
Cooking time: 7 minutes

Ingredients:

- 1-pound asparagus
- 1 teaspoon olive oil
- ½ teaspoon ground coriander

Directions:

1. Sprinkle asparagus with ground coriander and olive oil. Mix the vegetables gently and put them in the air fryer.
2. Cook the asparagus for 5 minutes at 400F.
3. Stir the vegetables and cook them for 2 additional minutes.

Nutrition value/serving: calories 118, fat 6.7, fiber 3.3, carbs 6.7, protein 10.9

Turmeric Cauliflower Florets

Servings: 2 | **Prep time:** 10 minutes
Cooking time: 15 minutes

Ingredients:

- 1 cup cauliflower florets
- 1 egg, beaten
- ½ teaspoon ground turmeric
- 1 teaspoon olive oil
- ½ teaspoon curry powder

Directions:

1. Mix cauliflower florets with ground turmeric and curry powder.
2. Dip every cauliflower floret in a beaten egg.
3. Brush the air fryer basket with olive oil and arrange the cauliflower florets inside.
4. Cook the vegetables at 365°F for 5 minutes on each side.

Nutrition value/serving: calories 136, fat 11.3, fiber 3.4, carbs 6.4, protein 4.6

Fenugreek Mushroom Caps

Servings: 4 | **Prep time:** 10 minutes
Cooking time: 11 minutes

Ingredients:

- 14 oz cremini mushroom caps
- 1 tablespoon fenugreek seeds
- 1 tablespoon olive oil
- ½ teaspoon lemon juice

Directions:

1. In the mixing bowl, combine olive oil, lemon juice, and fenugreek seeds.
2. Brush every mushroom cap with the oil mixture and arrange them in the air fryer basket.
3. Cook the mushrooms for 11 minutes at 380°F, stirring them every 3 minutes.

Nutrition value/serving: calories 61, fat 3.8, fiber 0.2, carbs 4.4, protein 2.8

Eggplant Rounds

Servings: 2 | **Prep time:** 15 minutes
Cooking time: 6 minutes

Ingredients:

- 2 eggplants, sliced
- ½ teaspoon sage
- ½ teaspoon dried cilantro
- ½ teaspoon dried oregano
- 1 tablespoon olive oil
- ½ teaspoon salt

Directions:

1. Mix eggplants and salt and leave the mixture for 10 minutes.
2. Dry the eggplants from juice and sprinkle with sage, dried cilantro, oregano, and olive oil.
3. Place the vegetables in the air fryer and cook for 6 minutes at 400F. Stir the eggplants after 4

minutes of cooking.

Nutrition value/serving: calories 92, fat 7.4, fiber 2.2, carbs 6.7, protein 2.4

Black Pepper White Beans

Servings: 4 | **Prep time:** 10 minutes
Cooking time: 7 minutes

Ingredients:

- 13 oz white beans, canned, drained
- 2 eggs, beaten
- 1 teaspoon salt
- ½ teaspoon ground black pepper
- 1 tablespoon olive oil

Directions:

1. Mix white beans with salt and ground black pepper.
2. Dip the vegetables into the beaten egg.
3. Shake the beans and place them in the air fryer in one layer.
4. Sprinkle them with olive oil and cook for 7 minutes at 395F. Stir the white beans after 5 minutes of cooking.

Nutrition value/serving: calories 100, fat 3, fiber 4.2, carbs 14.6, protein 5.1

Sweet Potato Bites

Servings: 4 | **Prep time:** 10 minutes
Cooking time: 4 minutes

Ingredients:

- 3 sweet potatoes, boiled
- ½ cup coconut flour
- ½ teaspoon salt
- ½ teaspoon ground black pepper
- 2 eggs, beaten
- 1 teaspoon ground paprika

Directions:

1. Mash the sweet potatoes and combine them with salt, ground black pepper, and ground paprika.
2. Form the small bites from the sweet potato mixture and dip them in the eggs.
3. Coat each bite in coconut flour and transfer it to the air fryer.
4. Cook the sweet potato bites for 2 minutes on each side at 400F. The cooked sweet potato bites should be golden brown.

Nutrition value/serving: calories 105, fat 2.9, fiber 1.4, carbs 5.1, protein 4.3

Zucchini Bites

Servings: 2 | **Prep time:** 10 minutes
Cooking time: 8 minutes

Ingredients:

- 1 zucchini, peeled
- ½ teaspoon garlic powder
- Cooking spray

Directions:

1. Cut the zucchini into small bites and sprinkle them with garlic powder and cooking spray.
2. Place the eggplants in the air fryer.
3. Cook the vegetables for 8 minutes at 375F.

Nutrition value/serving: calories 151, fat 6.5, fiber 8.2, carbs 15, protein 11.5

Ginger Pineapple

Servings: 4 | **Prep time:** 5 minutes
Cooking time: 5 minutes

Ingredients:

- 10 oz pineapple, roughly chopped
- ½ teaspoon ground ginger
- 1 teaspoon olive oil

Directions:

1. Mix up pineapple with olive oil and put it in the air fryer.
2. Sprinkle the fruits with ground ginger and cook for 3 minutes at 400F.
3. Flip the pineapple on another side and cook for 2 additional minutes.

Nutrition value/serving: calories 46, fat 1.2, fiber 1, carbs 9.5, protein 0.4

Crunchy Mushrooms

Servings: 2 | **Prep time:** 10 minutes
Cooking time: 6 minutes

Ingredients:

- 1 cup mushrooms
- 2 eggs, beaten
- 1/3 cup coconut flour
- 1 teaspoon olive oil
- ¼ teaspoon dried marjoram

Directions:

1. Mix coconut flour with dried marjoram.
2. Dip each mushroom in the egg, then coat in coconut flour.

3. Place the mushrooms in the air fryer in one layer and sprinkle with olive oil.
4. Cook them for 3 minutes on each side at 400°F. The cooked coated mushrooms will be light brown.

Nutrition value/serving: calories 162, fat 7.7, fiber 1.2, carbs 14.5, protein 9.1

Thyme Green Beans

Servings: 5 | **Prep time:** 10 minutes
Cooking time: 15 minutes

Ingredients:

- 8 oz green beans
- 11 tablespoons dried thyme
- ½ teaspoon salt
- 1 tablespoon olive oil

Directions:

1. Sprinkle the green beans with salt and thyme.
2. Brush the beans with olive oil gently and place them in the air fryer.
3. Cook the vegetables for 15 minutes at 355F. Flip green beans after 10 minutes of cooking.

Nutrition value/serving: calories 283, fat 21.7, fiber 1.5, carbs 3.9, protein 17.6

Tofu and Sweet Potatoes

Servings: 1 | **Prep time:** 10 minutes
Cooking time: 20 minutes

Ingredients:

- 1 sweet potato
- ½ teaspoon olive oil
- ¼ teaspoon salt
- ½ teaspoon ground black pepper
- ¼ cup tofu, shredded
- ½ teaspoon chives, chopped
- ½ teaspoon Greek yogurt

Directions:

1. Coat sweet potato with olive oil and sprinkle with salt and ground black pepper.
2. Place it in the air fryer and cook for 20 minutes at 350F.
3. Place the cooked sweet potato on the plate and mash it gently.
4. Sprinkle the sweet potato with tofu, chives, and Greek yogurt.

Nutrition value/serving: calories 125, fat 10.1, fiber 0.4, carbs 1.4, protein 7.3

Salty Zucchini

Servings: 4 | **Prep time:** 5 minutes
Cooking time: 25 minutes

Ingredients:

- 2 cups zucchini, roughly chopped
- 1 teaspoon salt
- 2 tablespoons olive oil

Directions:

1. Mix zucchini with salt and olive oil.
2. Place the vegetables in the air fryer and cook them for 25 minutes at 355°F or until the zucchini are golden brown. Stir the vegetables every 5 minutes.

Nutrition value/serving: calories 146, fat 8.4, fiber 3, carbs 16.3, protein 2.2

Garlic Patties

Servings: 4 | **Prep time:** 20 minutes
Cooking time: 4 minutes

Ingredients:

- 3 garlic cloves, peeled, diced
- 1 teaspoon olive oil
- ¼ teaspoon Italian seasonings
- 5 oz yeast rolls dough, diabetic-friendly
- 1 egg yolk
- ¼ cup mashed sweet potato
- Cooking spray

Directions:

1. Pour the olive oil into the pan.
2. Add garlic and Italian seasonings.
3. Cook the garlic for 5-6 minutes over medium heat or until the garlic is soft.
4. Mix garlic with mashed sweet potato.
5. Roll out the dough and cut it into 4 circles.
6. Place the garlic mixture on each dough piece and fold it into the patties.
7. Whisk the egg yolk.
8. Brush the patties with egg yolk and sprinkle with cooking spray.
9. Place the patties in the air fryer and cook them for 2 minutes on each side at 400F or until the patties are golden brown.

Nutrition value/serving: calories 171, fat 6.9, fiber 2.2, carbs 22.7, protein 4

Vegetable Meals

Crunchy Eggplants

Servings: 7 | **Prep time:** 10 minutes
Cooking time: 5 minutes

Ingredients:

- 3 eggplants, trimmed
- 1 teaspoon chili flakes
- 1 tablespoon olive
- ½ teaspoon salt

Directions:

1. Slice the eggplants and sprinkle them with salt.
2. Squeeze the eggplants from excess juice and dry them with a paper towel.
3. Sprinkle the vegetables with chili flakes and oil. Stir well and place in the air fryer.
4. Cook eggplants for 5 minutes at 400F. Shake the vegetables every 2 minutes to avoid burning.

Nutrition value/serving: calories 30, fat 2.1, fiber 0.9, carbs 2.8, protein 1

Sweet Potato Tots

Servings: 4 | **Prep time:** 15 minutes
Cooking time: 11 minutes

Ingredients:

- 1 sweet potato, peeled, grated
- 1/3 cup coconut flour
- ½ teaspoon ground black pepper
- 1 egg, beaten
- ½ teaspoon salt
- 1 teaspoon sunflower oil

Directions:

1. Mix grated sweet potato with ground black pepper, egg, and salt.
2. Add coconut flour and stir again.
3. Form the small tots from the prepared mixture.
4. Brush the air fryer basket with sunflower oil and place the sweet potato tots inside.
5. Cook them for 11 minutes at 390F. Flip the tots after 6 minutes of cooking.

Nutrition value/serving: calories 129, fat 7.1, fiber 0.9, carbs 10, protein 6.6

Tomatillos Salsa

Servings: 2 | **Prep time:** 10 minutes
Cooking time: 10 minutes

Ingredients:

- 1 cup tomatillos
- ½ cup fresh parsley, chopped
- ½ teaspoon minced garlic
- 1 teaspoon olive oil
- 1 jalapeno pepper, trimmed

Directions:

1. Place the jalapeno pepper and tomatillos in the air fryer.
2. Cook the vegetables for 10 minutes at 375F.
3. Transfer the cooked tomatillos and jalapeno to the blender.
4. Add minced garlic, olive oil, and fresh parsley, then blend the mixture until smooth.
5. Blend the mixture until smooth.
6. Transfer the cooked salsa to the serving bowl.

Nutrition value/serving: calories 23, fat 0.5, fiber 1.5, carbs 4.4, protein 0.9

Cinnamon Baby Carrots

Servings: 2 | **Prep time:** 5 minutes
Cooking time: 12 minutes

Ingredients:

- 1 cup baby carrots
- 1 teaspoon olive oil
- 1 teaspoon almond flour
- ½ teaspoon ground cinnamon

Directions:

1. Mix baby carrots with ground cinnamon and olive oil.
2. Put the vegetables in the air fryer and cook at 400F for 8 mutes.
3. Add almond flour and stir gently.
4. Cook the baby carrots for 5 minutes more.

Nutrition value/serving: calories 25, fat 0.4, fiber 1.7, carbs 4.9, protein 0.2

Dill Sweet Potatoes

Servings: 2 | **Prep time:** 15 minutes
Cooking time: 10 minutes

- 2 sweet potatoes
- 1 teaspoon fresh dill, chopped
- 2 teaspoons avocado oil
- 1 teaspoon salt

Directions:

1. Cut the sweet potatoes into Hasselback.
2. Sprinkle them with avocado oil and salt and place them in the air fryer.
3. Cook the vegetables for 25 minutes at 360F or

until the sweet potatoes are soft.
4. Sprinkle the hot sweet potatoes with dill.

Nutrition value/serving: calories 42, fat 4.7, fiber 0.1, carbs 0.4, protein 0

Pumpkin Fries

Servings: 4 | **Prep time:** 10 minutes
Cooking time: 10 minutes

Ingredients:
- 5 oz pumpkin, peeled, sliced
- 3 tablespoons coconut flour
- 1 egg, beaten
- ½ teaspoon ground black pepper

Directions:
1. Dip the pumpkin slices in an egg and sprinkle with ground black pepper.
2. Coat every pumpkin slice in coconut flour.
3. Place the coated vegetables in the air fryer in one layer.
4. Cook the fries at 400°F for 5 minutes on each side. The cooked pumpkin fries will be golden brown.

Nutrition value/serving: calories 54, fat 1.2, fiber 0.9, carbs 8.9, protein 2.4

Green Beans Hash

Servings: 2 | **Prep time:** 10 minutes
Cooking time: 20 minutes

Ingredients:
- 1-pound green beans, chopped, boiled
- ½ teaspoon salt
- ½ teaspoon ground coriander
- 1 tablespoon sesame oil

Directions:
1. Place the green beans on the foil.
2. Sprinkle the ingredients with salt, ground coriander, and sesame oil. Stir, then wrap the foil.
3. Place the wrapped vegetables in the air fryer and cook for 20 minutes at 360F.

Nutrition value/serving: calories 230, fat 7.3, fiber 7.4, carbs 31.5, protein 10.7

Yogurt Zucchini

Servings: 2 | **Prep time:** 10 minutes
Cooking time: 15 minutes

Ingredients:
- 2 zucchini, roughly chopped
- 4 tablespoons Greek yogurt
- ¼ teaspoon dried basil
- ½ teaspoon olive oil
- ¼ teaspoon salt

Directions:
1. Place the zucchini in the air fryer basket.
2. Sprinkle the vegetables with olive oil, basil, and salt. Add yogurt and mix the ingredients well.
3. Cook them for 15 minutes at 385F.

Nutrition value/serving: calories 191, fat 4.8, fiber 5.1, carbs 34.2, protein 3.8

Okra and Garlic Balls

Servings: 4 | **Prep time:** 10 minutes
Cooking time: 6 minutes

Ingredients:
- 1-pound okra chopped
- 2 eggs, beaten
- 1 teaspoon minced garlic
- ½ cup almond flour
- ½ teaspoon salt
- 1 teaspoon olive oil

Directions:
1. Combine the chopped okra with salt, minced garlic, and beaten eggs.
2. Then coat the okra in the almond flour and transfer it to the air fryer. Flatten the vegetables in one layer and sprinkle with olive oil.
3. Cook the meal at 365°F for 3 minutes on each side.

Nutrition value/serving: calories 132, fat 3.3, fiber 4.3, carbs 18.4, protein 6.8

Broccoli Fries

Servings: 4 | **Prep time:** 10 minutes
Cooking time: 10 minutes

Ingredients:
- 2 cups broccoli, roughly chopped
- 1 tablespoon chili powder
- 1 tablespoon olive oil

Vegetable Meals | 71

Directions:

1. Sprinkle the broccoli with chili powder and olive oil.
2. Shake the vegetables well and place them in the air fryer.
3. Cook the fries at 375F for 5 minutes.
4. Stir the broccoli well and cook for 5 more minutes.

Nutrition value/serving: calories 36, fat 0.8, fiber 2.3, carbs 7.2, protein 0.8

Cinnamon Apple Wedges

Servings: 4 | **Prep time:** 10 minutes
Cooking time: 10 minutes

Ingredients:

- 4 apples
- 1 tablespoon apple pie spices
- 1 teaspoon ground cinnamon

Directions:

1. Cut the apples into small wedges and sprinkle them with ground cinnamon and apple pie spices.
2. Shake the fruits well.
3. Transfer the apple wedges to the air fryer and cook for 10 minutes at 345°F, stirring occasionally.

Nutrition value/serving: calories 131, fat 1.7, fiber 5.6, carbs 31.8, protein 0.7

Paprika Slices

Servings: 4 | **Prep time:** 10 minutes
Cooking time: 12 minutes

Ingredients:

- 2 eggplants, sliced
- 1 tablespoon Greek yogurt
- 1 tablespoon ground paprika
- 1 teaspoon avocado oil
- ½ teaspoon lemon juice

Directions:

1. In the shallow bowl, combine yogurt, ground paprika, avocado oil, and lemon juice.
2. Brush the eggplant slices with the yogurt mixture on both sides.
3. Place the eggplant slices in the air fryer in one layer and cook them at 390°F for 2 minutes on each side.
4. Repeat the same steps with the remaining eggplants.

Nutrition value/serving: calories 97, fat 3, fiber 9.7, carbs 17.3, protein 2.9

Roasted Jalapeno

Servings: 2 | **Prep time:** 10 minutes
Cooking time: 16 minutes

Ingredients:

- 2 jalapeno peppers
- 1 tablespoon avocado oil
- 1 teaspoon lemon juice
- ½ teaspoon minced garlic

Directions:

1. Pierce the jalapeno peppers and coat them with cooking spray.
2. Place the peppers in the air fryer and cook them at 400°F for 8 minutes on each side.
3. Mix avocado oil with lemon juice and minced garlic to make the dressing.
4. Peel the cooked peppers carefully and remove the seeds.
5. Chop the jalapeno peppers roughly and sprinkle with the garlic dressing.

Nutrition value/serving: calories 36, fat 0.9, fiber 2.3, carbs 6.6, protein 1.1

Lemongrass Bites

Servings: 4 | **Prep time:** 20 minutes
Cooking time: 10 minutes

Ingredients:

- 1 ¼ teaspoons green curry paste
- ½ teaspoon ground turmeric
- ¼ teaspoon minced garlic
- ¼ teaspoon lemongrass
- ¼ onion, diced
- 1 teaspoon olive oil
- ½ teaspoon salt
- 1 carrot, boiled
- 1 cup broccoli, boiled
- 1 egg white, whisked
- 1 teaspoon sesame oil

Directions:

1. Blend all the ingredients together until smooth.
2. Form small bites from the mixture with the help of a spoon. If the vegetable mixture is sticky,

add more almond flour.
3. Place the veggie bites inside the air fryer in one layer.
4. Cook the veggie bites for 10 minutes at 390F.

Nutrition value/serving: calories 108, fat 6.3, fiber 1.4, carbs 10.4, protein 2.6

Beans Peppers

Servings: 4 | **Prep time:** 10 minutes
Cooking time: 15 minutes

Ingredients:

- 4 bell peppers
- ¼ cup black beans, canned
- ½ teaspoon salt
- ½ teaspoon ground paprika
- ½ teaspoon chili flakes

Directions:

1. Remove the seeds from the bell peppers.
2. In the mixing bowl, combine black beans, salt, ground paprika, and chili flakes.
3. Fill the bell peppers with the bean mixture and wrap every bell pepper in foil.
4. Cook the bell peppers for 15 minutes at 365F.

Nutrition value/serving: calories 174, fat 0.6, fiber 3.9, carbs 5.2, protein 5.6

Asparagus Fries

Servings: 6 | **Prep time:** 10 minutes
Cooking time: 7 minutes

Ingredients:

- 1-pound asparagus, roughly chopped
- 1 teaspoon garlic powder
- 1 tablespoon olive oil
- 3 eggs, beaten
- ½ cup almond flour

Directions:

1. In a bowl, mix eggs with garlic powder.
2. Dip the asparagus into the egg mixture, then coat them in almond flour.
3. After this, dip the asparagus in the eggs and coat in the remaining almond flour.
4. Place the asparagus in the air fryer basket, sprinkle with olive oil, and bake for 7 minutes at 400F or until the asparagus is golden.

Nutrition value/serving: calories 144, fat 5.7, fiber 3, carbs 14.5, protein 9.1

Zucchini Cubes

Servings: 6 | **Prep time:** 10 minutes
Cooking time: 10 minutes

Ingredients:

- 1-pound zucchini, cubed
- 1 teaspoon chili flakes
- 1 tablespoon Plain yogurt
- ½ teaspoon ground black pepper
- 1 teaspoon olive oil
- ½ teaspoon salt

Directions:

1. Mix zucchini cubes with salt.
2. Place the vegetables in the air fryer and sprinkle with olive oil and ground black pepper.
3. Cook the zucchini for 5 minutes at 400F.
4. Stir the vegetables well and cook for 5 more minutes.
5. In the shallow bowl, whisk chili flakes with Plain yogurt.
6. Place the cooked pumpkin cubes on the plates and sprinkle with yogurt-chili dressing.

Nutrition value/serving: calories 65, fat 1.4, fiber 2.4, carbs 13.7, protein 1.4

Chickpea Balls

Servings: 6 | **Prep time:** 10 minutes
Cooking time: 4 minutes

Ingredients:

- 1 cup chickpeas, canned, rinsed
- 2 tablespoons fresh dill, chopped
- ½ garlic clove, diced
- 1 tablespoon almond flour
- 1 teaspoon sesame seeds
- ¼ teaspoon ground paprika
- 3 tablespoons lemon juice
- 1 teaspoon olive oil

Directions:

1. Blend the chickpeas, dill, garlic, paprika, and lemon juice in the blender until smooth.
2. Transfer the mixture to the mixing bowl.
3. Add sesame seeds, almond flour, and olive oil. Stir the mixture.
4. Form the small balls from it.
5. Arrange the balls in one layer and cook at 400°F for 2 minutes on each side.

Nutrition value/serving: calories 148, fat 3.1, fiber 6, carbs 2.3, protein 6.9

Cilantro Cakes

Servings: 6 | **Prep time:** 15 minutes
Cooking time: 6 minutes

- 8 oz Phyllo dough
- 2 cups fresh cilantro, chopped
- 1 cup low-fat cottage cheese
- ½ cup Mozzarella, shredded
- 2 eggs, beaten
- 1 teaspoon salt
- 1 teaspoon olive oil
- ¼ cup of water

Directions:

1. Mix chopped cilantro with cottage cheese, Mozzarella, eggs, and salt.
2. Brush the air fryer basket with olive oil.
3. Divide Phyllo dough into 2 parts.
4. Place the first part of the dough in the air fryer.
5. Place the cottage cheese mixture on it.
6. Top the mixture with the remaining Phyllo dough and brush it with water and olive oil.
7. Cook the pie for 6 minutes at 400F or until the pie is golden brown.

Nutrition value/serving: calories 223, fat 9.2, fiber 0.9, carbs 2.2, protein 12.5

Coconut Cucumbers

Servings: 2 | **Prep time:** 10 minutes
Cooking time: 10 minutes

Ingredients:

- 1 cup cucumber, sliced
- 4 tablespoons coconut flour
- 1 egg, beaten
- ¼ cup coconut cream

Directions:

1. Mix coconut flour with egg and cream.
2. Brush the cucumbers with egg mixture.
3. Arrange the cucumbers in the air fryer in one layer and cook at 395°F for 2 minutes on each side.
4. Repeat the same steps with the remaining cucumbers.

Nutrition value/serving: calories 277, fat 16.3, fiber 1.9, carbs 1.7, protein 22.7

Parsley Artichoke Hearts

Servings: 4 | **Prep time:** 10 minutes
Cooking time: 13 minutes

Ingredients:

- 4 artichoke hearts, canned
- 1 tablespoon mayonnaise, sugar-free
- 1 teaspoon mustard
- 1 teaspoon dried parsley
- 1/3 cup coconut flour
- 1 teaspoon avocado oil

Directions:

1. Mix mayonnaise with mustard and dried parsley.
2. Brush the artichoke hearts carefully with a mayonnaise mixture and then coat them with coconut flour.
3. Sprinkle the coated artichoke hearts with avocado oil and place them in the air fryer.
4. Cook the artichokes for 13 minutes at 400F or until they are crunchy.

Nutrition value/serving: calories 133, fat 2.4, fiber 8.4, carbs 24.9, protein 6.8

Sweet Potato Croquettes

Servings: 4 | **Prep time:** 10 minutes
Cooking time: 5 minutes

Ingredients:

- ½ cup mashed sweet potato
- ¼ cup fresh dill, chopped
- ¼ cup white beans, cooked
- 2 tablespoons almond flour
- ½ teaspoon salt
- 1 teaspoon onion powder
- 1 teaspoon sesame oil

Directions:

1. Blend the dill and white beans until smooth.
2. Combine mashed sweet potato, blended dill, and white beans in the mixing bowl.
3. Add almond flour, salt, and onion powder.
4. Form the croquettes from the mixture.
5. Brush the air fryer basket with sesame oil and place the prepared croquettes inside.
6. Cook the meal for 5 minutes at 395F or until it is golden brown.

Nutrition value/serving: calories 93, fat 2.4, fiber 2.6, carbs 14.4, protein 3.8

Garlic Snap Peas

Servings: 2 | **Prep time:** 5 minutes
Cooking time: 15 minutes

Ingredients:

- 1 cup snap peas
- ½ teaspoon garlic powder
- ½ teaspoon olive oil

Directions:

1. Mix snap peas with garlic powder and olive oil.
2. Line the air fryer basket with baking paper.
3. Arrange the snap peas on the baking paper in one layer.
4. Cook the chips at 360F for 10 minutes.
5. Flip them on another side and cook for 5 minutes more at 400F or until the chips are crunchy.

Nutrition value/serving: calories 71, fat 1.5, fiber 3.7, carbs 11, protein 4

Onion Cakes

Servings: 2 | **Prep time:** 10 minutes
Cooking time: 8 minutes

Ingredients:

- ½ cup corn kernels, frozen
- 1 egg, beaten
- 1 tablespoon Greek yogurt
- 4 tablespoons coconut flour
- ½ onion, minced
- ½ teaspoon salt
- ½ teaspoon ground black pepper
- 1 tablespoon fresh parsley, chopped
- 1 teaspoon sunflower oil

Directions:

1. In the big bowl, mix corn kernels with egg, Greek yogurt, coconut flour, onion, salt, ground black pepper, and parsley. You should get a thick and non-sticky mixture.
2. Form the small fritters from the corn mixture.
3. Place the fritters in the air fryer and gently sprinkle them with sunflower oil.
4. Cook the meal for 4 minutes from each side at 375F.

Nutrition value/serving: calories 159, fat 5.5, fiber 2.3, carbs 22.6, protein 6.1

Mushroom Steak

Servings: 2 | **Prep time:** 10 minutes
Cooking time: 6 minutes

Ingredients:

- 2 large Portobello mushroom caps
- ½ teaspoon minced onion
- ½ teaspoon cayenne pepper
- ½ teaspoon salt
- 2 teaspoons olive oil

Directions:

1. Beat the mushroom caps with the kitchen mallet gently.
2. In the shallow bowl, mix the minced onion with cayenne pepper, salt, and olive oil.
3. Place the mushroom caps in the air fryer and brush them well with an olive oil mixture.
4. Cook the mushroom steaks for 6 minutes at 400F.

Nutrition value/serving: calories 29, fat 0.7, fiber 1.3, carbs 3.7, protein 3.2

Tofu Burgers

Servings: 4 | **Prep time:** 15 minutes
Cooking time: 10 minutes

Ingredients:

- ½ cup almond flour
- 2 eggs, beaten
- ¼ cup tofu, shredded
- 2 cups mushrooms, grinded
- 1 teaspoon garlic powder
- 1 teaspoon curry powder
- ½ teaspoon salt
- 1 tablespoon avocado oil

Directions:

1. Mix eggs with almond flour, tofu, mushrooms, garlic powder curry powder, and salt.
2. Brush the air fryer basket with avocado oil.
3. Form the small burgers from the mixture and place them in the air fryer.
4. Cook the burgers at 400°F for 5 minutes on each side.

Nutrition value/serving: calories 131, fat 5.8, fiber 1.4, carbs 12.6, protein 7.6

Spinach Rolls

Servings: 2 | **Prep time:** 10 minutes
Cooking time: 15 minutes

Ingredients:

- ½ eggplants, peeled
- 1 bell pepper, trimmed
- 1 teaspoon avocado oil
- ½ teaspoon onion powder
- 1 teaspoon dried parsley
- ½ teaspoon salt
- 1 tablespoon coconut cream
- ½ teaspoon lime juice
- 4 spinach leaves

Directions:

1. Place the eggplant and bell pepper in the air fryer. Pierce them and sprinkle them with avocado oil.
2. Cook the vegetables for 15 minutes at 395F. Flip them on another side during cooking 2 times.
3. Mix the cream with salt, lime juice, dried parsley, and onion powder.
4. Chop the cooked vegetables and combine them with the cream mixture.
5. Put two spinach leaves together.
6. Place the vegetable mixture on the prepared spinach leaves and roll them into wraps.
7. Repeat the same steps with the remaining spinach leaves.

Nutrition value/serving: calories 82, fat 3.1, fiber 5.8, carbs 13.8, protein 2.1

Stuffed Zucchini

Servings: 4 | **Prep time:** 15 minutes
Cooking time: 15 minutes

Ingredients:

- Small zucchini
- 4 teaspoon pecans, chopped
- ½ teaspoon minced ginger
- 1 garlic clove, diced
- ½ teaspoon ground turmeric
- ½ teaspoon ground paprika
- 1 tablespoon fresh parsley, chopped
- 1 tablespoon olive oil
- 1 tablespoon lemon juice

Directions:

1. In the mixing bowl, combine chopped pecans, minced ginger, garlic, ground turmeric, paprika, parsley, olive oil, and lemon juice. Stir it well.
2. Make the cut cross in each zucchini.
3. Fill the zucchini with pecan mixture and transfer to the air fryer.
4. Cook the zucchini for 10 minutes at 360F.
5. Check the zucchini, flip them on another side if needed, and cook for 5 more minutes. The cooked zucchini will be tender.

Nutrition value/serving: calories 188, fat 6.1, fiber 19.8, carbs 33.3, protein 6.3

Beans Balls

Servings: 2 | **Prep time:** 20 minutes
Cooking time: 6 minutes

Ingredients:

- 10 oz white beans, canned, drained
- 1 tablespoon tomato paste
- ¼ onion, diced
- 1 teaspoon olive oil

Directions:

1. In the mixing bowl, combine onion, tomato paste, white beans, and olive oil.
2. Form the small balls from the mixture.
3. Place the balls in the air fryer and cook them for 3 minutes on each side at 400F.

Nutrition value/serving: calories 118, fat 8.7, fiber 1.4, carbs 6.6, protein 5

Cheese Chickpeas

Servings: 4 | **Prep time:** 10 minutes
Cooking time: 15 minutes

Ingredients:

- 2 cups chickpeas, canned, drained
- 1 teaspoon ground paprika
- 1 teaspoon olive oil
- ½ cup Mozzarella, shredded

Directions:

1. Mix chickpeas with ground paprika and olive oil and place in the air fryer basket.
2. Cook the meal for 15 minutes at 350F. Stir the chickpeas after 7 minutes of cooking and sprinkle with Mozzarella.

Nutrition value/serving: calories 79, fat 3.3, fiber 4, carbs 12.9, protein 1.5

Onion Quesadillas

Servings: 2 | **Prep time:** 15 minutes
Cooking time: 5 minutes

Ingredients:

- 2 corn tortillas
- ½ cup white beans, canned, drained
- ½ red onion, diced
- ¼ teaspoon minced garlic
- 1 tablespoon Greek yogurt
- 1 tablespoon lemon juice
- 2 teaspoons olive oil
- 2 tablespoons fresh cilantro, chopped
- ¼ cup corn kernels, canned

Directions:

1. In the mixing bowl, combine white beans, corn kernels, onion, fresh cilantro, and minced garlic.
2. In the shallow bowl, whisk together lemon juice and Greek yogurt.
3. Brush the corn tortillas with a Greek yogurt mixture.
4. Place the white bean mixture on one part of each tortilla and fold them.
5. Secure the tortillas with toothpicks and brush them with olive oil.
6. Place the quesadillas in the air fryer and cook them for 5 minutes at 400F.

Nutrition value/serving: calories 376, fat 13.7, fiber 10.1, carbs 48, protein 17.8

Cauliflower Fritters

Servings: 4 | **Prep time:** 10 minutes
Cooking time: 15 minutes

Ingredients:

- 1 cup zucchini, shredded
- 4 eggs, beaten
- 1 teaspoon ground black pepper
- 1 tablespoon Greek yogurt
- ½ teaspoon salt
- ½ teaspoon olive oil

Directions:

1. Whisk together shredded zucchini and eggs.
2. Add ground black pepper, yogurt, and salt.
3. Brush the air fryer basket with olive oil and pour the cauliflower mixture inside.
4. Cook the mixture for 15 minutes at 385F.
5. Then cut the meal into small fritters.

Nutrition value/serving: calories 136, fat 9.9, fiber 0.7, carbs 2.6, protein 9.7

Turmeric Corn

Servings: 2 | **Prep time:** 9 minutes
Cooking time: 15 minutes

Ingredients:

- 2 corns on the cob
- 1 teaspoon salt
- ½ teaspoon ground turmeric
- 2 tablespoons sesame oil

Directions:

1. Brush the corn on the cob with sesame oil.
2. Sprinkle it with salt and ground turmeric.
3. Place the corn in the air fryer and cook it for 10 minutes at 365F.
4. Flip it on another side and cook for 5 more minutes.

Nutrition value/serving: calories 278, fat 17, fiber 0.1, carbs 12.2, protein 4.6

Beans Muffins

Servings: 2 | **Prep time:** 10 minutes
Cooking time: 7 minutes

Ingredients:

- ¼ cup white beans, canned
- 1 tablespoon almond flour
- ½ teaspoon baking powder
- 1 egg, beaten
- 1 tablespoon cut oats
- ½ teaspoon ground paprika
- ¼ teaspoon salt
- 1 tablespoon olive oil

Directions:

1. Mash the white beans until you get a puree.
2. Combine the white beans puree and almond flour.
3. Add baking powder, egg, cut oats, ground paprika, and salt.
4. Stir and make the smooth batter.
5. Grease the muffin molds with olive oil generously.
6. Fill each muffin mold with batter halfway and arrange them in the air fryer.
7. Cook the muffins for 7 minutes at 395°F. The

muffins are cooked when they are light brown.

Nutrition value/serving: calories 126, fat 8.3, fiber 1.5, carbs 5.4, protein 4.6

Arugula Salad

Servings: 2 | **Prep time:** 10 minutes
Cooking time: 10 minutes

Ingredients:

- ½ cup cherry tomatoes halved
- 2 cups arugula, chopped
- 1 tablespoon lemon juice
- 1 tablespoon avocado oil
- 4 oz firm tofu, cubed
- 1 tablespoon curry paste
- ¼ teaspoon sesame oil

Directions:

1. Sprinkle the tofu cubes with curry paste and sesame oil.
2. Place it in the air fryer and cook at 400°F for 5 minutes on each side.
3. In the salad bowl, combine cherry tomatoes, arugula, lemon juice, and avocado oil. Stir the salad well.
4. Top the salad with tofu and stir it only before serving.

Nutrition value/serving: calories 75, fat 4, fiber 1.7, carbs 4.3, protein 6.2

Cashew Pizza

Servings: 4 | **Prep time:** 10 minutes
Cooking time: 20 minutes

Ingredients:

- 4 oz Pizza dough, diabetic-friendly
- 1 teaspoon tomato sauce, sugar-free
- ½ teaspoon dried oregano
- ¼ teaspoon lemon juice
- 1 teaspoon olive oil
- 2 Kalamata olives, sliced
- 2 tablespoons cashew, chopped
- ¼ teaspoon garlic powder

Directions:

1. Mix tomato sauce with dried oregano, lemon juice, and olive oil to make pizza sauce.
2. Brush the pizza dough with pizza sauce well.
3. Sprinkle the pizza dough with sliced olives.
4. Top the pizza with garlic powder and chopped cashews.
5. Place the pizza in the air fryer and cook it for 20 minutes at 355F or until the pizza dough is golden brown.

Nutrition value/serving: calories 184, fat 12.3, fiber 1.8, carbs 6.9, protein 2.9

Dill Parsnip

Servings: 5 | **Prep time:** 15 minutes
Cooking time: 20 minutes

Ingredients:

- 1-pound parsnip, peeled
- 1 tablespoon apple cider vinegar
- 1 teaspoon olive oil
- ½ teaspoon dried dill
- ¼ teaspoon salt

Directions:

1. Cut the parsnip into the fries shape.
2. In the shallow bowl, mix olive oil with dill and apple cider vinegar.
3. Sprinkle the parsnip fries with the vinegar mixture and place in the air fryer.
4. Cook the fries for 10 minutes at 360F.
5. Stir the parsnip fries well and cook them for 10 additional minutes.
6. Sprinkle the cooked hot parsnip fries with salt.

Nutrition value/serving: calories 89, fat 0.5, fiber 5.7, carbs 6.6, protein 1.4

DESSERTS

Desserts

Vegetable Bars

Servings: 6 | **Prep time:** 25 minutes
Cooking time: 14 minutes

Ingredients:

- 1 teaspoon dried yeast
- 2 tablespoons Erythritol
- ½ cup Greek yogurt
- 10 oz almond flour
- 1 cup rutabaga, chopped
- 1 teaspoon olive oil

Directions:

1. Place rutabaga in the saucepan. Stir well and leave for 10 minutes.
2. Combine dried yeast, Erythritol, and Greek yogurt.
3. Add almond flour and knead soft dough. Place dough in a warm place and leave for 10-15 minutes.
4. Bring the rutabaga to a boil and simmer it for 5 minutes over low heat.
5. Then cool the rutabaga mixture completely.
6. Roll out the dough and cut it into 6 pieces.
7. Place the rutabaga mixture on each dough piece and fold them into the scones. Secure the edges of the scones.
8. Brush each rutabaga scone with olive oil and transfer it to the air fryer.
9. Cook the rutabaga scones at 355°F for 7 minutes on each side.

Nutrition value/serving: calories 238, fat 1.6, fiber 2, carbs 4.9, protein 6.1

Sweet Zucchini Pie

Servings: 6 | **Prep time:** 15 minutes
Cooking time: 30 minutes

Ingredients:

- ½ cup Erythritol
- 2 zucchini, grated
- 3 eggs, beaten
- ½ teaspoon ground nutmeg
- 1 cup almond flour
- 1 teaspoon vanilla extract

Directions:

1. Blend Erythritol and almond flour until smooth and fluffy.
2. Add eggs and blend the mixture until homogenous.
3. Add flour, vanilla extract, and ground nutmeg.
4. Stir the mixture well and add the zucchini. Stir it until homogenous.
5. Line the baking pan with parchment and pour the zucchini batter inside.
6. Place the baking pan in the air fryer
7. Cook the zucchini pie for 30 minutes at 355F.

Nutrition value/serving: calories 178, fat 2.4, fiber 0.9, carbs 2.4, protein 5

Chocolate Muffins

Servings: 4 | **Prep time:** 15 minutes
Cooking time: 8 minutes

Ingredients:

- 4 oz sugar-free dark chocolate, chopped
- 2 eggs, beaten
- 4 teaspoons olive oil
- 4 teaspoons almond flour
- 4 teaspoons Splenda

Directions:

1. Melt the chocolate in the microwave completely.
2. Combine melted chocolate with olive oil and stir until you get a smooth liquid mixture.
3. Add beaten eggs and Splenda.
4. Add almond flour and stir the batter until homogenous.
5. Pour the batter into the muffin molds or ramekins and arrange them in the air fryer.
6. Cook the chocolate muffins for 8 minutes at 375F.
7. Let the cooked dessert cool for 5 minutes before serving.

Nutrition value/serving: calories 243, fat 14.4, fiber 1.2, carbs 23, protein 5.4

Matcha Cookies

Servings: 6 | **Prep time:** 15 minutes
Cooking time: 12 minutes

Ingredients:

- 1 teaspoon matcha powder
- ¾ cup almonds, chopped
- 3 tablespoons olive oil
- ½ cup almond flour

- 2 tablespoons Erythritol

Directions:
1. In the big bowl, combine matcha powder and almond flour.
2. In a separate bowl, combine olive oil and Erythritol. Whisk until fluffy.
3. Combine the oil mixture and almond flour mixture.
4. Add almonds and knead the soft non-sticky dough.
5. Form the small balls (cookies) from the dough.
6. Line the air fryer with baking paper and place the cookies inside.
7. Cook them at 350F for 12 minutes. The time of cooking depends on the cookie size.

Nutrition value/serving: calories 212, fat 14.9, fiber 2.2, carbs 5.7, protein 5.9

Vanilla Bombs

Servings: 6 | **Prep time:** 15 minutes
Cooking time: 7 minutes

Ingredients:
- 4 eggs
- ½ cup Splenda
- 7 oz almond flour
- 1 teaspoon vanilla extract
- ½ teaspoon avocado oil

Directions:
1. Crack eggs and separate the egg yolks from egg whites.
2. Mix Splenda with egg yolks. Whisk the mixture until it turns into lemon color.
3. Whisk the egg whites till you get strong peaks.
4. Combine the egg yolk mixture and almond flour. Stir until homogenous.
5. Incorporate vanilla extract and egg whites.
6. Brush the muffin molds with avocado oil, then pour the biscuit mixture into the molds.
7. Transfer them to the air fryer.
8. Cook the vanilla bombs for 7 minutes at 375F or until they are light brown.
9. Let the cooked vanilla bombs cool for 10 minutes and remove them from the molds.

Nutrition value/serving: calories 289, fat 7.6, fiber 1.9, carbs 4.3, protein 10.9

Coconut Sandwich

Servings: 4 | **Prep time:** 15 minutes
Cooking time: 30 minutes

Ingredients:
- 1 cup almond flour
- 4 tablespoons Erythritol
- 3 tablespoons avocado oil
- ½ teaspoon baking powder
- 1 teaspoon lime juice
- 2 tablespoons cocoa powder
- ¼ cup coconut cream
- ¼ cup of ice cubes

Directions:
1. In the mixing bowl, combine almond flour and cocoa powder.
2. Add baking powder, lime juice, and avocado oil and knead the dough.
3. Form 8 balls from the dough.
4. Line the air fryer basket with parchment and place the dough balls inside in one layer.
5. Press the balls a little and cook them for 14 minutes at 350°F. Repeat the same steps with the rest of the balls.
6. Blend coconut cream and ice cubes until it is smooth and thick. Add Erythritol to ice cream during cooking.
7. Scoop the ice cream and place it on the 4 cookies.
8. Cover them with the remaining cookies to get sandwiches.

Nutrition value/serving: calories 348, fat 20.1, fiber 1.7, carbs 8.5, protein 4.5

Cinnamon Cookies

Servings: 4 | **Prep time:** 15 minutes
Cooking time: 8 minutes

Ingredients:
- 1 sheet sugar-free diabetic-friendly dough
- 1 tablespoon olive oil
- 1 tablespoon Erythritol
- 1 tablespoon ground cinnamon
- ½ teaspoon ground nutmeg

Directions:
1. Roll out the dough a little.
2. Then sprinkle it with olive oil.
3. In the shallow bowl, combine Erythritol, ground cinnamon, and ground nutmeg.

4. Sprinkle the dough with the cinnamon mixture on one side. Brush the mixture to even it out if needed.
5. Then roll up the dough and slice it.
6. Press the side to the middle of each slice a little to get the shape of "elephant ears".
7. Transfer the cookies to the air fryer in one layer.
8. Cook the cookies for 8 minutes at 365F.
9. Flip the cookies on another side after 6 minutes of cooking.

Nutrition value/serving: calories 98, fat 6.7, fiber 1.3, carbs 5.7, protein 0.9

Walnut Cookies

Servings: 6 | Prep time: 15 minutes
Cooking time: 8 minutes

Ingredients:

- 1 cup almond flour
- ¼ cup Greek yogurt
- 1 egg, beaten
- 1 teaspoon vanilla extract
- 3 tablespoons Erythritol
- 2 oz walnuts, chopped
- 1 teaspoon chia seeds
- 1 teaspoon baking powder
- ½ teaspoon lemon zest, grated
- 1 tablespoon olive oil

Directions:

1. In the mixing bowl, combine all ingredients and knead the soft dough with the help of the fingertips.
2. Cut the dough into 6 pieces and roll them out in the shape of "fingers".
3. Line the air fryer basket with baking paper and arrange the finger cookies inside.
4. Cook the cookies at 365°F for 4 minutes on each side.

Nutrition value/serving: calories 207, fat 10.2, fiber 1.6, carbs 2.8, protein 6.3

Cocoa Cookies

Servings: 4 | Prep time: 10 minutes
Cooking time: 7 minutes

Ingredients:

- 4 tablespoons almond flour
- 2 tablespoons Greek yogurt
- 2 tablespoons Erythritol
- 2 tablespoons cocoa powder
- 1 oz sugar-free chocolate chips
- ½ teaspoon vanilla extract
- 2 tablespoons olive oil
- ¾ teaspoon ground cardamom

Directions:

1. In the mixing bowl, combine all ingredients and knead the soft and non-sticky dough.
2. Form the log from the dough and cut it into equal pieces.
3. Make the balls from the dough pieces.
4. Line the air fryer with baking paper and arrange the dough balls inside.
5. Cook the cookies for 7 minutes at 350F.

Nutrition value/serving: calories 168, fat 9.6, fiber 1.8, carbs 9.1, protein 2.2

Vanilla Clouds

Servings: 6 | Prep time: 10 minutes
Cooking time: 45 minutes

Ingredients:

- 2 egg whites
- ½ cup Erythritol
- 1 teaspoon lime juice
- 1 teaspoon vanilla extract

Directions:

1. Whisk the egg whites till they have soft peaks.
2. Add Erythritol, vanilla extract, and lime juice and whisk the egg whites till you get the strong peaks.
3. Line the air fryer basket with parchment.
4. With a spoon or using a pastry bag, make the small meringues on the parchment.
5. Cook the "clouds" at 310F for 45 minutes.

Nutrition value/serving: calories 67, fat 0, fiber 0.1, carbs 1.8, protein 1.2

Almond Clouds

Servings: 4 | Prep time: 10 minutes
Cooking time: 40 minutes

Ingredients:

- 1 egg white
- 4 tablespoons almond flakes
- 2 tablespoons Erythritol
- ½ teaspoon vanilla extract

Directions:

1. Mix egg white with vanilla extract and Erythritol and whisk the mixture till you get the strong peaks.
2. Slowly incorporate almond flakes into the mixture.
3. Line the air fryer basket with baking paper.
4. Form the "clouds" from the mixture and place them in the air fryer.
5. Cook the almond clouds for 40 minutes at 330F or until the "clouds" are light brown.

Nutrition value/serving: calories 47, fat 1.7, fiber 0.5, carbs 9.8, protein 1.1

Pecan Cookies

Servings: 12 | **Prep time:** 30 minutes
Cooking time: 30 minutes

Ingredients:

- 9 oz almond flour
- 1 teaspoon vanilla extract
- 1 egg, beaten
- 2 tablespoons avocado oil
- 5 pecans, chopped
- 2 tablespoons Erythritol

Directions:

1. Add vanilla extract, avocado oil ground cardamom, and Erythritol to the almond flour.
2. Add egg and chopped pecans, then knead the dough.
3. Form 12 balls from the dough. Refrigerate them for 20 minutes.
4. Make the crosses on the surface of each cookie with the fork.
5. Place the cookies in the air fryer and cook them for 15 minutes at 350F.
6. Repeat the same steps with the remaining dough balls.

Nutrition value/serving: calories 108, fat 3, fiber 1.9, carbs 7.3, protein 2.1

Cinnamon Yucca Fries

Servings: 6 | **Prep time:** 10 minutes
Cooking time: 25 minutes

Ingredients:

- 1-pound yucca root, peeled
- 1 teaspoon ground cinnamon
- 1 teaspoon avocado oil
- 1 cup water, for cooking

Directions:

1. Cut the yucca root into the fries and place it in the saucepan.
2. Add water and bring the fries to a boil.
3. Boil the yucca fries for 20 minutes.
4. Drain the water and dry the yucca fries.
5. Transfer them to the air fryer and sprinkle with avocado oil.
6. Fry the fries at 400°F for 2 minutes on each side.
7. Transfer the cooked yucca fries to the plate and sprinkle with ground cinnamon.

Nutrition value/serving: calories 141, fat 1, fiber 1.4, carbs 3.7, protein 1.2

Almond Biscuits

Servings: 15 | **Prep time:** 15 minutes
Cooking time: 10 minutes

Ingredients:

- ½ cup ground almond
- 1 cup almond flour
- 1 teaspoon baking powder
- 1 teaspoon lemon juice
- ¼ cup of Erythritol
- 4 tablespoons avocado oil
- ½ cup almonds, whole

Directions:

1. In the mixing bowl, combine ground almond, almond flour, baking powder, lemon juice, Erythritol, and avocado oil.
2. Knead the dough and form 15 balls from it.
3. Top every ball with whole almond nut and press them in gently.
4. Place the balls in the air fryer and cook for 10 minutes at 360F or until the biscuits are light brown.

Nutrition value/serving: calories 172, fat 11.9, fiber 1.4, carbs 4.4, protein 3.2

Blackberry Skewers

Servings: 2 | **Prep time:** 10 minutes
Cooking time: 3 minutes

Ingredients:

- ½ mango, peeled
- 1 cup blackberries
- 1 teaspoon Plain yogurt
- ¼ teaspoon ground cinnamon

Directions:
1. Chop the mango roughly and string it and the blackberries on the metal skewers.
2. Place the fruit skewers in the air fryer and cook them for 3 minutes at 365F.
3. Sprinkle the hot-cooked fruit skewers with yogurt and ground cinnamon.

Nutrition value/serving: calories 126, fat 0.8, fiber 3.6, carbs 3.5, protein 1.9

Tasty Fries

Servings: 4 | Prep time: 10 minutes
Cooking time: 10 minutes

Ingredients:
- 2 cups jicama fries, frozen
- 1 tablespoon Erythritol
- 1 teaspoon ground nutmeg
- 1 teaspoon avocado oil

Directions:
1. Place the jicama fries in the air fryer and sprinkle them with avocado oil.
2. Bake the fries for 10 minutes at 385F. Shake the jicama fries every 2 minutes to avoid burning.
3. In the shallow bowl, combine ground nutmeg and Erythritol.
4. When the fries are cooked, transfer them to the big bowl and sprinkle them with a sweet nutmeg mixture.
5. Stir the fries well.

Nutrition value/serving: calories 48, fat 1.2, fiber 3.8, carbs 7.9, protein 0.5

RECIPE INDEX

A

almonds
  Almond Clouds, 82
  Almond Biscuits, 83

apples
  Cinnamon Apple Wedges, 72
  Cinnamon Apples, 28

apricots
  Apricot Fritters, 16

arugula
  Arugula Salad, 78

asparagus
  Asparagus Omelette, 18
  Thyme Asparagus, 28
  Coriander Asparagus, 67
  Asparagus Fries, 73
  Garlic Asparagus, 33

avocado
  Avocado Cups, 17
  Avocado Canoes, 21

B

bagels
  Cherry Tomato Pizzas, 19

beef
  Paprika Meatballs, 12
  Meat Roll, 21
  Paprika Beef Bars, 23
  Beef Wraps, 27
  Beef Rolls, 17
  Beef and Eggs, 20
  Garlic Duck Meatballs, 62

bell peppers
  Parsley Kebabs, 29
  Beans Peppers, 73

blackberries
  Blackberry Skewers, 83

blue mussels
  Paprika and Basil Mussels, 47

broccoli
  Avocado Cups, 17
  Broccoli and Sauce Bites, 22
  Dill Broccoli Rice, 31
  Buffalo Style Broccoli, 33
  Lime Broccoli, 66
  Carrot Mix, 66
  , 71
  Broccoli Wings, 28

Brussels sprouts
  Carrot Mix, 66
  Black Pepper Brussels Sprout Halves, 29
  Cumin Brussels Sprouts, 35

C

cabbage
  Lemon Purple Cabbage, 34
  Turmeric Cabbage Wedges, 35

calamari
  Turmeric Calamari Rings, 42
  Cayenne Calamari Rings, 46
  Calamari and Sweet Potato Balls, 48

carrot
  Carrot Mix, 66
  Garlic and Carrot Puree, 34
  Cinnamon Baby Carrots, 70

catfish fillet
  Cumin Catfish, 41

cauliflower
  Hot Cakes, 27
  Garlic Cauliflower, 31
  Paprika Cauliflower Rice, 32
  Turmeric Cauliflower Florets, 67
  Garlic Cauliflower Head, 67

celery root
  Celery Chicken Thighs, 58

cherry tomatoes
  Chicken and Tofu Pizza, 61
  Cherry Tomato Pizzas, 19
  Tomato Chicken Wings, 59

chicken
  Chicken and Mushrooms Muffins, 12
  Paprika Meatballs, 12
  Chicken Chimichangas, 18
  Coriander Chicken Fillets, 20
  Chicken Pockets, 21
  Wrapped Chicken, 21
  Lime Chicken, 52
  Paprika Chicken Drumsticks, 52
  Chili Pepper Chicken Meatballs, 52
  Nutmeg Tenders, 52
  Tomato Wings, 53
  Italian Seasonings Chicken Thighs, 53
  Rosemary Whole Chicken, 53
  Cumin Chicken Breast, 53
  Chives Patties, 54
  Chicken Breast Boats, 54
  Greens Wraps, 57
  Mustard Chicken Tenders, 57
  Jalapeno Chicken Tights, 58
  Celery Chicken Thighs, 58
  Jalapeno Chicken Tights, 58
  Celery Chicken Thighs, 58
  Tender Chicken Breas, 58
  Oregano Chicken Sausage, 59
  Thyme and Garlic Whole Chicken, 59
  Tomato Chicken Wings, 59
  Greek Style Chicken Breast, 60
  Fenugreek and Dill Chicken, 60
  Chicken and Tofu Pizza, 61
  Fragrant Whole Chicken, 61
  Spicy Chicken, 55
  Chicken and Asparagus, 59
  Dill Chicken Cutlets, 61

Recipe Index | 85

Onion Chicken, 54
Oregano Chicken Fillets, 55
Marjoram Chicken Shred, 55
Coated Chicken, 55
Yellow Fillets, 56
Egg Chicken Fillets, 56
Tender Chicken Strips, 56
Cucumber and Chicken Sandwich, 57
Almond Chicken Tenders, 58
Chicken and Onion Bowl, 59
Oats Chicken Balls, 60
Hot Chili Flakes Chicken, 60
Mustard and Mayo Chicken, 62
Parsley Liver Pate, 53
Garlic Chicken, 55
Yogurt Chicken Wings, 57
Oregano and Chicken Meatballs, 22

chickpeas
Cilantro and Chickpea Fritters, 33
Chickpea Balls, 73
Cheese Chickpeas, 76

chili flakes
Fried Feta, 14
Crushed Eggs, 22
Zucchini Cubes, 73

chili pepper
Oregano and Chicken Meatballs, 22
Chili Poppers, 63

coconut
Coconut Cucumbers, 74

coconut cream
Coconut Duck Cream, 62
Coconut Sandwich, 81

cod
Chili Cod en Papilote, 40
Garlic Fish Cakes, 49

Cod Balls, 13
Cod Patties, 38
Spinach Cod, 40
Cilantro Cod, 42
Chili Cod Fillets, 43
Cod Balls, 43
Olives and Cod, 46
Basil Cod, 48
Sweet and Sour Cod, 49

corn kernels
Onion Cakes, 75

corn tortillas
Chicken Chimichangas, 18
Gyros, 20
Chili Fish Tacos, 50
Chicken and Asparagus, 59

cottage cheese
Cottage Cheese Eggs, 13
Cheese Sandwich, 17
Wonton Crab Meat, 22
Coriander Portobello Caps, 34

crab meat
Wonton Crab Meat, 22
Paprika Crab Cakes, 38
Chili Crab Bites, 41

crayfish
Parsley Crayfish, 48

cremini mushrooms
Chicken and Mushrooms Muffins, 12

cucumber
Gyros, 20
Chicken and Kalamata Olives, 56
Coconut Cucumbers, 74

D
dorado
Lime Dorado, 46

duck
Coriander Duck Breast, 61

Oregano Duck Drumsticks, 61
Coconut Duck Cream, 62
Garlic Duck Meatballs, 62
Cayenne Pepper Duck Wings, 62
Chili Poppers, 63

E
eggplants
Turmeric Eggplant Fries, 27
Chili Eggplant Coins, 30
Eggplant Rounds, 67
Crunchy Eggplants, 70

eggs
Thyme Asparagus, 28
Oregano Eggs, 15
Turmeric Eggs, 15
Garlic Eggs, 16
Nutmeg Eggs, 18
Crushed Eggs, 22

F
Feta cheese
Fried Feta, 14

fresh cilantro
Cilantro Casserole, 19
Coriander Sardines, 47
Cilantro Cakes, 74

G
garlic
Garlic Patties, 69
Appetizer Garlic Bulbs, 32
Garlic Fish Cakes, 49
Thyme and Garlic Whole Chicken, 59

Greek yogurt
Apricot Fritters, 16

green beans
Garlic Green Beans, 30
Thyme Green Beans, 69
Green Beans Hash, 71

green cabbage
  Chili Fish Tacos, 50

J

jalapeno peppers
  Roasted Jalapeno, 72

K

Kalamata olives
  Chicken and Kalamata Olives, 56

kale
  Kale Cakes, 16
  Sweet and Sour Cod, 49

L

lemon
  Nutmeg Tilapia, 41
  Jalapeno Chicken Tights, 58

lemon juice
  Garlic Shrimps, 38

lemongrass
  Lemongrass Bites, 72

lettuce
  Chicken and Kalamata Olives, 56

lime
  Basil Cod, 48

lime juice
  Parsley Kebabs, 29
  Lime Snapper, 46

lobster
  Coriander Lobster Tails, 38
  Onion Lobsters, 45

M

mackerel
  Tender Mackerel, 40

Mozzarella
  Spinach Pie, 13
  Stuffed Tortillas, 14
  Cheese Sandwich, 17
  Cauliflower Mix, 27

mushrooms
  Fenugreek Mushroom Caps, 67
  Mushroom Stea, 75
  Nutmeg Mushrooms, 26
  Crunchy Mushrooms, 68
  Tofu Burgers, 75

O

okra
  Okra and Garlic Balls, 71

P

parsnip
  Dill Parsnip, 78

pecans
  Lime Broccoli, 66
  Stuffed Zucchini, 76
  Pecan Cookies, 83

pineapple
  Ginger Pineapple, 68

potatoes
  Dill Potato, 26
  Curry Fries, 26
  Chili Wedges, 28
  Cauliflower Mix, 27

pumpkin
  Pumpkin Fries, 71

R

radish
  Radish Hash, 30

red onion
  Onion Quesadillas, 77

rutabaga
  Vegetable Bars, 80

S

salmon fillet
  Lime Salmon, 39
  Fish Spring Rolls, 45

sardines
  Coriander Sardines, 47
  Cumin Grilled Sardines, 47
  Zucchini Sardines, 49

scallions
  Avocado Canoes, 21

scallops
  Nutmeg Scallops, 44
  Oregano Scallops, 46

sea bass
  Cumin Sea Bass, 42
  Garlic Seabass, 43

sea scallops
  Paprika Scallops, 45

shrimps
  Carrot Rolls, 14
  Garlic Shrimps, 38
  Italian Seasoning Shrimps, 39
  Cinnamon Shrimps, 44
  Rosemary Shrimps, 44

snap peas
  Garlic Snap Peas, 75

spaghetti squash
  Thyme Spaghetti Squash, 34

spinach
  Nutmeg Eggs, 18
  Spinach Cod, 40
  Cucumber and Chicken Sandwich, 57
  Spinach and Turkey Mix, 63
  Spinach Rolls, 76

sweet potatoes
  Thyme Muffins, 16
  Zucchini Burgers, 32
  Calamari and Sweet Potato Balls, 48
  Tofu and Sweet Potatoes, 69
  Sweet Potato Tots, 70
  Sweet Potato Croquettes, 74
  Sweet Potato Fries, 26
  Sweet Potato Bites, 68
  Dill Sweet Potatoes, 70

T

tilapia
- Nutmeg Tilapia, 41
- Fish Quesadillas, 19
- Coriander Tilapia Fillets, 39
- Coriander Tilapia Sticks, 40
- Tilapia Cream, 43
- Nutmeg Bites, 45

tofu
- Tofu Burgers, 75
- Arugula Salad, 78

tomatillos
- Tomatillos Salsa, 70

tomatoes
- Tomato Wings, 53

tortillas
- Stuffed Tortillas, 14

turkey
- Sage Turkey, 54

W

walnuts
- Walnut Cookies, 82

white beans
- Avocado Patties, 31
- Black Pepper White Beans, 68
- Beans Balls, 76
- Beans Muffins, 77

white cabbage
- Sage Shredded Cabbage, 34

white onion
- Cilantro Casserole, 19
- Radish Hash, 30
- Chicken and Onion Bowl, 59

white rice
- Soy Sauce Rice, 29

Y

yellow onion
- Beef and Eggs, 20
- Dill Squids, 42

yogurt
- Kale Cakes, 16
- Asparagus Omelette, 18
- Chicken Pockets, 21
- Garlic Cauliflower Head, 67
- Yogurt Zucchini, 71
- Paprika Slices, 72

yucca root
- Cinnamon Yucca Fries, 83

Z

zucchini
- Zucchini Burgers, 32
- Parsley Zucchini, 32
- Zucchini Bites, 68
- Salty Zucchini, 69
- Yogurt Zucchini, 71
- Zucchini Cubes, 73
- Stuffed Zucchini, 76
- Cauliflower Fritters, 77
- Sweet Zucchini Pie, 80